LETTER TO A FRIEND

HYDRIOTAPHIA

THE GARDEN OF CYRUS

Sir Thomas Browne

British Library Cataloguing in Publication Data

A catalogue record for this book is available from the British Library

ISBN-13: 978-1-911405-90-0

Cover Illustration:
Funeral of a Roman Emperor.
Giovanni Lanfranco (c. 1636)

CONTENTS

TO A
FRIEND,

Upon occasion of the
Death of his Intimate Friend.

Give me leave to wonder that News of this nature should have such heavy Wings, that you should hear so little concerning your dearest Friend, and that I must make that unwilling Repetition to tell you, *Ad portam rigidos calces extendit,* that he is Dead and Buried, and by this time no Puny among the mighty Nations of the Dead; for tho he left this World not very many days past, yet every hour you know largely addeth unto that dark Society; and considering the incessant Mortality of Mankind, you cannot conceive there dieth in the whole Earth so few as a thousand an hour.

Altho at this distance you had no early Account or Particular of his Death; yet your Affection may cease to wonder that you had not some secret Sense or Intimation thereof by Dreams, thoughtful Whisperings, Mercurisms, Airy Nuncio's, or sympathetical Insinuations, which many seem to have had at the Death of their dearest Friends: for since we find in that famous Story, that Spirits themselves were fain to tell their Fellows at a distance, that the great *Antonio* was dead; we have a sufficient Excuse for our Ignorance in such Particulars, and must rest content with the common Road, and *Appian* way of Knowledge by Information. Tho the uncertainty of the End of this World hath confounded all Humane Predictions; yet they who shall live to see the Sun and Moon darkned, and the Stars to fall from Heaven, will hardly be deceived in the Advent of the last Day; and therefore strange it is, that the common Fallacy of consumptive Persons, who feel not themselves dying, and therefore still hope to live, should also reach their Friends in perfect Health and Judgment. That you should be so little acquainted with *Plautus's* sick Complexion, or that almost an *Hippocratical* Face should not alarum you to higher fears, or rather despair of his Continuation in such an emaciated State, wherein medical Predictions fail not, as sometimes in acute Diseases, and wherein 'tis as dangerous to be sentenced by a Physician as a Judge.

Upon my first Visit I was bold to tell them who had not let fall all hopes of his Recovery, That in my sad Opinion he was not like to behold a Grashopper, much less to pluck another Fig; and in no long time after seemed to discover that odd mortal Symptom in him not mention'd by *Hippocrates*, that is, to lose his own Face and look like some of his near Relations; for he maintained not his proper Countenance, but looked like his Uncle, the Lines of whose Face lay deep and invisible in his healthful Visage before: for as from our beginning we run through variety of Looks, before we come to consistent and settled Faces; so before our End, by sick and languishing Alterations, we put on new Visages: and in our Retreat to Earth, may fall upon such Looks which from community of seminal Originals were before latent in us.

He was fruitlessly put in hope of advantage by change of Air, and imbibing the pure Aerial Nitre of these Parts; and therefore being so far spent, he quickly found *Sardinia* in *Tivoli*,[1] and the most healthful Air of little effect, where Death had set her Broad Arrow;[2] for he lived not unto the middle of May, and confirmed the Observation of *Hippocrates*[3] of that mortal time of the Year when the Leaves of the Fig-tree resemble a Daw's Claw. He is happily seated who lives in Places whose Air, Earth, and Water, promote not the Infirmities of his weaker Parts, or is early removed into Regions that correct them. He that is tabidly inclined, were unwise to pass his days in Portugal: Cholical Persons will find little Comfort in Austria or Vienna: He that is weak-legg'd must not be in Love with Rome, nor an infirm Head with Venice or Paris. Death hath not only particular Stars in Heaven, but malevolent Places on Earth, which single out our Infirmities, and strike at our weaker Parts; in which Concern, passager and migrant Birds have the great Advantages; who are naturally constituted for distant Habitations, whom no Seas nor Places limit, but in their appointed Seasons will visit us from Greenland and Mount Atlas, and as some think, even from the *Antipodes*.[4]

Tho we could not have his Life, yet we missed not our desires in his soft Departure, which was scarce an Expiration; and his End not unlike his Beginning, when the salient Point scarce affords a sensible motion, and his Departure so like unto Sleep, that he scarce needed the civil Ceremony of closing his Eyes; contrary unto the common way wherein Death draws up, Sleep lets fall the Eyelids. With what strift and pains we came into the World we know not; but 'tis commonly no easie matter to get out of it: yet if it could be made out, that such who have easie Nativities have commonly hard Deaths, and contrarily; his Departure was so easie, that we might justly suspect his Birth was of another nature, and that some Juno sat cross-legg'd at his Nativity.

Besides his soft Death, the incurable state of his Disease might somewhat extenuate your Sorrow, who know that Monsters but seldom happen, Miracles more rarely, in Physick.[5] *Angelus Victorius* gives a serious Account of a Consumptive, Hectical, Pthysical Woman, who was suddenly cured by the Intercession of *Ignatius*.[6] We read not of any in Scripture who in this case applied unto our Saviour, tho some may be contained in that large Expression, That he went about Galilee healing all manner of Sickness, and all manner of Diseases.[7] Amulets, Spells, Sigils and Incantations, practised in other Diseases, are seldom pretended in this; and we find no Sigil in the Archidoxis of Paracelsus to cure an extreme Consumption or *Marasmus*, which if other Diseases fail, will put a period unto long Livers, and at last make dust of all. And therefore the *Stoicks* could not but think that the firy Principle would wear out all the rest, and at last make an end of the World, which notwithstanding without such a lingring period the Creator may effect at his Pleasure: and to make an end of all things on Earth, and our Planetical System of the World, he need but put out the Sun.

I was not so curious to entitle the Stars unto any concern of his Death, yet could not but take notice that he died when the Moon was in motion from the Meridian; at which time, an old Italian long ago would persuade me, that the greatest part of Men died: but herein I confess I could never satisfie my Curiosity; altho from the time of Tides in Places upon or near the Sea, there may be considerable Deductions; and *Pliny*[8] hath an odd and remarkable Passage concerning the Death of Men and Animals upon the Recess or Ebb of the Sea. However, certain it is he died in the dead and deep part of the Night, when *Nox* might be most apprehensibly said to be the Daughter of *Chaos*, the Mother of Sleep and Death, according to old Genealogy; and so went out of this World about that hour when our blessed Saviour entred it, and about what time many conceive he will return again unto it. *Cardan* hath a peculiar and no hard Observation from a Man's hand, to know whether he was born in the day or night, which I confess holdeth in my own. And *Scaliger* to that purpose hath another from the tip of the Ear:[9] most Men are begotten in the Night, most Animals in the Day; but whether more Persons have been born in the Night or the Day, were a Curiosity undecidable, tho more have perished by violent Deaths in the Day; yet in natural Dissolutions both Times may hold an Indifferency, at least but contingent Inequality. The whole course of Time runs out in the Nativity and Death of Things; which whether they happen by Succession or Coincidence, are best computed by the natural, not artificial Day.

That Charles the Fifth was Crowned upon the day of his Nativity, it being in his own power so to order it, makes no singular Animadversion; but that he should also take King Francis Prisoner upon that day, was an unexpected Coincidence, which made the same remarkable. *Antipater* who had an Anniversary Fever every Year upon his Birth day, needed no Astrological Revolution to know what day he should dye on. When the fixed Stars have made a Revolution unto the points from whence they first set out, some of the Ancients thought the World would have an end; which was a kind of dying upon the day of its Nativity. Now the Disease prevailing and swiftly advancing about the time of his Nativity, some were of Opinion, that he would leave the World on the day he entred into it: but this being a lingring Disease, and creeping softly on, nothing critical was found or expected, and he died not before fifteen days after. Nothing is more common with Infants than to dye on the day of their Nativity, to behold the worldly Hours and but the Fractions thereof; and even to perish before their Nativity in the hidden World of the Womb, and before their good Angel is conceived to undertake them. But in Persons who out-live many Years, and when there are no less than three hundred sixty five days to determine their Lives in every Year; that the first day should make the last, that the Tail of the Snake should return into its Mouth precisely at that time, and they should wind up upon the day of their Nativity,[10] is indeed a remarkable Coincidence, which tho Astrology hath taken witty pains to salve, yet hath it been very wary in making Predictions of it.

In this consumptive Condition and remarkable Extenuation he came to be almost half himself, and left a great part behind him which he carried not to the Grave. And tho that Story of Duke *John Ernestus Mansfield* be not so easily swallowed,[11] that at his Death his Heart was found not to be so big as a Nut; yet if the Bones of a good Sceleton weigh little more than twenty pounds, his Inwards and Flesh remaining could make no Bouffage,[12] but a light bit for the Grave. I never more lively beheld the starved Characters of Dante in any living Face;[13] an *Aruspex* might have read a Lecture upon him without Exenteration, his Flesh being so consumed that he might, in a manner, have discerned his Bowels without opening of him: so that to be carried *sextâ cervice*[14] to his Grave, was but a civil unnecessity; and the Complements of the Coffin might out-weigh the Subject of it.

Omnibonus Ferrarius in mortal Dysenteries of Children[15] looks for a Spot behind the Ear; in consumptive Diseases some eye the Complexion of Moals; Cardan eagerly views the Nails, some the Lines of the Hand, the Thenar or Muscle of the Thumb; some are so curious as to observe the depth of the Throat-pit, how the proportion varieth of the Small of the Legs unto the Calf, or the compass of the Neck unto the Circumference of the Head: but all these, with many more, were so drowned in a mortal Visage and last Face of Hippocrates, that a weak Physiognomist might say at first eye, This was a Face of Earth, and that Morta[16] had set her Hard-Seal upon his Temples, easily perceiving what *Caricatura* Draughts[17] Death makes upon pined Faces, and unto what an unknown degree a Man may live backward.

Tho the Beard be only made a distinction of Sex and sign of masculine Heat by *Ulmus*,[18] yet the Precocity and early growth thereof in him, was not to be liked in reference unto long Life. Lewis, that virtuous but unfortunate King of Hungary, who lost his Life at the Battel of *Mohacz*, was said to be born without a Skin, to have bearded at Fifteen, and to have shewn some gray Hairs about Twenty; from whence the Diviners conjectured, that he would be spoiled of his Kingdom, and have but a short Life: But Hairs make fallible Predictions, and many Temples early gray have out-lived the Psalmist's Period.[19] Hairs which have most amused me have not been in the Face or Head, but on the Back, and not in Men but Children, as I long ago observed in that Endemial Distemper[20] of little Children in Languedock, called the *Morgellons*, wherein they critically break out with harsh Hairs on their Backs, which takes off the Unquiet Symptoms of the Disease, and delivers them from Coughs and Convulsions [21]

The Egyptian Mummies that I have seen, have had their Mouths open, and somewhat gaping, which affordeth a good opportunity to view and observe their Teeth, wherein 'tis not easie to find any wanting or decayed: and therefore in Egypt, where one Man practised but one Operation, or the Diseases but of single Parts, it must needs be a barren Profession to confine unto that of drawing of Teeth, and little better than to have been Tooth-drawer unto King Pyrrhus, who had but two in his Head.[22] How the *Bannyans* of India maintain the Integrity of those Parts, I find not particularly observed; who notwithstanding have an Advantage of their Preservation by abstaining from all Flesh, and employing their Teeth in such Food unto which they may seem at first framed, from their Figure and Conformation: but sharp and corroding Rheums had so early mouldered those Rocks and hardest parts of his Fabrick, that a Man might well conceive that his Years were never like to double or twice tell over his Teeth.[23] Corruption had dealt more severely with them, than sepulchral Fires and smart Flames with those of burnt Bodies of old; for in the burnt Fragments of Urns which I have enquired into, altho I seem to find few Incisors or Shearers, yet the Dog Teeth and Grinders do notably resist those Fires.[24]

In the Years of his Childhood he had languished under the Disease of his Country, the Rickets; after which notwithstanding many I have seen become strong and active Men; but whether any have attained unto very great Years the Disease is scarce so old as to afford good Observations. Whether the Children of the English Plantations be subject unto the same Infirmity, may be worth the observing. Whether Lameness and Halting do still encrease among the Inhabitants of Rovigno in Istria, I know not; yet scarce twenty Years ago Monsieur Du Loyr observed, that a third part of that People halted: but too certain it is, that the Rickets encreaseth among us; the Small-Pox grows more pernicious than the Great: the Kings Purse knows that the King's Evil grows more common. *Quartan* Agues are become no strangers in Ireland; more common and mortal in England: and tho the Ancients gave that Disease very good Words,[25] yet now that Bell makes no strange sound which rings out for the Effects thereof.[26]

Some think there were few Consumptions in the Old World, when Men lived much upon Milk; and that the ancient Inhabitants of this Island were less troubled with Coughs when they went naked, and slept in Caves and Woods, than Men now in Chambers and Feather-beds. Plato will tell us, that there was no such Disease as a Catarrh in Homer's time, and that it was but new in Greece in his Age. Polydore Virgil delivereth that Pleurisies were rare in England, who lived but in the days of Henry the Eighth. Some will allow no Diseases to be new, others think that many old ones are ceased; and that such which are esteemed new, will have but their time: However, the Mercy of God hath scattered the great heap of Diseases, and not loaded any one Country with all: some may be new in one Country which have been old in another. New Discoveries of the Earth discover new Diseases: for besides the common swarm, there are endemial and local Infirmities proper unto certain Regions, which in the whole Earth make no small number: and if *Asia, Africa*, and *America* should bring in their List, *Pandora's Box* would swell, and there must be a strange Pathology.

Most Men expected to find a consumed Kell,[27] empty and bladder-like Guts, livid and marbled Lungs, and a withered *Pericardium* in this exuccous Corps: but some seemed too much to wonder that two Lobes of his Lungs adhered to his side; for the like I had often found in bodies of no suspected Consumptions or difficulty of Respiration. And the same more often happeneth in Men than other Animals; and some think, in Women than in Men: but the most remarkable I have met with, was in a Man,[28] after a Cough of almost fifty Years, in whom all the Lobes adhered unto the Pleura, and each Lobe unto another; who having also been much troubled with the Gout, brake the Rule of Cardan,[29] and died of the Stone in the Bladder. Aristotle makes a Query, Why some Animals cough as Man, some not, as Oxen. If coughing be taken as it consisteth of a natural and voluntary motion, including Expectoration and spitting out, it may be as proper unto Man as bleeding at the Nose; otherwise we find that Vegetius and Rural Writers have not left so many Medicines in vain against the Coughs of Cattel; and Men who perish by Coughs dye the Death of Sheep, Cats and Lyons: and tho Birds have no Midriff, yet we meet with divers Remedies in Arrianus against the Coughs of Hawks. And tho it might be thought, that all Animals who have Lungs do cough; yet in cetaceous Fishes, who have large and strong Lungs, the same is not observed; nor yet in oviparous Quadrupeds: and in the greatest thereof, the Crocodile, altho we read much of their Tears, we find nothing of that motion.

From the Thoughts of Sleep, when the Soul was conceived nearest unto Divinity, the Ancients erected an Art of Divination, wherein while they too widely expatiated in loose and inconsequent Conjectures, Hippocrates[30] wisely considered Dreams as they presaged Alterations in the Body, and so afforded hints toward the preservation of Health, and prevention of Diseases; and therein was so serious as to advise Alteration of Diet, Exercise, Sweating, Bathing and Vomiting; and also so religious, as to order Prayers and Supplications unto respective Deities, in good Dreams unto *Sol, Jupiter cúlestis, Jupiter opulentus, Minerva, Mercurius*, and *Apollo*; in bad unto *Tellus* and the Heroes.

And therefore I could not but take notice how his Female Friends were irrationally curious so strictly to examine his Dreams, and in this low state to hope for the Fantasms of Health. He was now past the healthful Dreams of the Sun, Moon, and Stars in their Clarity and proper Courses. 'Twas too late to dream of Flying, of Limpid Fountains, Smooth Waters, white Vestments, and fruitful green Trees, which are the Visions of healthful Sleeps, and at good distance from the Grave.

And they were also too deeply dejected that he should dream of his dead Friends, inconsequently divining, that he would not be long from them; for strange it was not that he should sometimes dream of the dead whose Thoughts run always upon Death: beside, to dream of the dead, so they appear not in dark Habits, and take no thing away from us, in Hippocrates his Sense was of good signification: for we live by the dead, and every thing is or must be so before it becomes our Nourishment. And Cardan, who dream'd that he discoursed with his dead Father in the Moon, made thereof no mortal Interpretation: and even to dream that we are dead, was no condemnable Fantasm in old *Oneirocriticism*, as having a signification of Liberty, vacuity from Cares, exemption and freedom from Troubles, unknown unto the dead.

Some Dreams I confess may admit of easie and feminine Exposition: he who dream'd that he could not see his right Shoulder, might easily fear to lose the sight of his right Eye; he that before a Journey dream'd that his Feet were cut off, had a plain warning not to undertake his intended Journey. But why to dream of Lettuce should presage some ensuing Disease, why to eat Figs should signifie foolish Talk, why to eat Eggs great Trouble, and to dream of Blindness should be so highly commended, according to the *Oneirocritical* Verses of Astrampsychus and Nicephorus, I shall leave unto your Divination.

He was willing to quit the World alone and altogether, leaving no Earnest behind him for Corruption or Aftergrave, having small content in that common satisfaction to survive or live in another, but amply satisfied that his Disease should dye with himself, nor revive in a Posterity to puzzle Physick, and make sad Memento's of their Parent hereditary. Leprosie awakes not sometimes before Forty, the Gout and Stone often later; but consumptive and tabid[31] Roots sprout more early, and at the fairest make seventeen Years of our Life doubtful before that Age. They that enter the World with original Diseases as well as Sin, have not only common Mortality but sick Traductions to destroy them, make commonly short Courses, and live not at length but in Figures; so that a sound *Cæsarean* Nativity[32] may out-last a natural Birth, and a Knife may sometimes make way for a more lasting fruit than a Midwife; which makes so few Infants now able to endure the old Test of the River,[33] and many to have feeble Children who could scarce have been married at Sparta, and those provident States who studied strong and healthful Generations; which happen but contingently in mere pecuniary Matches, or Marriages made by the Candle,[34] wherein notwithstanding there is little redress to be hoped from an Astrologer or a Lawyer, and a good discerning Physician were like to prove the most successful Counsellor.

Julius Scaliger, who in a sleepless Fit of the Gout could make two hundred Verses in a Night, would have but five plain Words upon his Tomb.[35] And this serious Person, tho no minor Wit, left the Poetry of his Epitaph unto others; either unwilling to commend himself, or to be judged by a Distich, and perhaps considering how unhappy great Poets have been in versifying their own Epitaphs; wherein Petrarcha, Dante, and Ariosto, have so unhappily failed, that if their Tombs should out-last their Works, Posterity would find so little of Apollo on them, as to mistake them for *Ciceronian* Poets.

In this deliberate and creeping progress unto the Grave, he was somewhat too young, and of too noble a mind, to fall upon that stupid Symptom observable in divers Persons near their Journeys end, and which may be reckoned among the mortal Symptoms of their last Disease; that is, to become more narrow minded, miserable and tenacious, unready to part with any thing when they are ready to part with all, and afraid to want when they have no time to spend; mean while Physicians, who know that many are mad but in a single depraved Imagination, and one prevalent Desipiency; and that beside and out of such single Deliriums a Man may meet with sober Actions and good Sense in Bedlam; cannot but smile to see the Heirs and concerned Relations, gratulating themselves in the sober departure of their Friends; and tho they behold such mad covetous Passages, content to think they dye in good Understanding, and in their sober Senses.

Avarice, which is not only Infidelity but Idolatry, either from covetous Progeny or questuary Education, had no Root in his Breast, who made good Works the Expression of his Faith, and was big with desires unto publick and lasting Charities; and surely where good Wishes and charitable Intentions exceed Abilities, Theorical Beneficency may be more than a Dream. They build not Castles in the Air who would build Churches on Earth; and tho they leave no such Structures here, may lay good Foundations in Heaven. In brief, his Life and Death were such, that I could not blame them who wished the like, and almost to have been himself; almost, I say; for tho we may wish the prosperous Appurtenances of others, or to be an other in his happy Accidents; yet so intrinsecal is every Man unto himself, that some doubt may be made, whether any would exchange his Being, or substantially become another Man.

He had wisely seen the World at home and abroad, and thereby observed under what variety Men are deluded in the pursuit of that which is not here to be found. And altho he had no Opinion of reputed Felicities below, and apprehended Men widely out in the estimate of such Happiness; yet his sober contempt of the World wrought no Democritism or Cynicism, no laughing or snarling at it, as well understanding there are not Felicities in this World to satisfie a serious Mind; and therefore to soften the stream of our Lives, we are fain to take in the reputed Contentations of this World, to unite with the Crowd in their Beatitudes, and to make our selves happy by Consortion, Opinion, or Co-existimation: for strictly to separate from received and customary Felicities, and to confine unto the rigor of Realities, were to contract the Consolation of our Beings unto too uncomfortable Circumscriptions.

Not to fear Death, nor desire it,[36] was short of his Resolution: to be dissolved, and be with Christ, was his dying ditty. He conceived his Thred long, in no long course of Years, and when he had scarce out-lived the second life of Lazarus[37]; esteeming it enough to approach the Years of his Saviour, who so ordered his own humane State, as not to be old upon Earth.

But to be content with Death may be better than to desire it: a miserable Life may make us wish for Death, but a virtuous one to rest in it; which is the advantage of those resolved Christians, who looking on Death not only as the sting, but the period and end of Sin, the Horizon and Isthmus between this Life and a better, and the Death of this World but as a Nativity of another, do contentedly submit unto the common Necessity, and envy not Enoch or Elias.

Not to be content with Life is the unsatisfactory state of those which destroy themselves;[38] who being afraid to live, run blindly upon their own Death, which no Man fears by Experience: and the Stoicks had a notable Doctrine to take away the fear thereof; that is, In such Extremities to desire that which is not to be avoided, and wish what might be feared; and so made Evils voluntary, and to suit with their own Desires, which took off the terror of them.

But the ancient Martyrs were not encouraged by such Fallacies; who, tho they feared not Death, were afraid to be their own Executioners; and therefore thought it more Wisdom to crucifie their Lusts than their Bodies, to circumcise than stab their Hearts, and to mortifie than kill themselves.

His willingness to leave this World about that Age when most Men think they may best enjoy it, tho paradoxical unto worldly Ears, was not strange unto mine, who have so often observed, that many, tho old, oft stick fast unto the World, and seem to be drawn like Cacus's Oxen, backward with great strugling and reluctancy unto the Grave. The long habit of Living makes meer Men more hardly to part with Life, and all to be nothing, but what is to come. To live at the rate of the old World, when some could scarce remember themselves young, may afford no better digested Death than a more moderate period. Many would have thought it an Happiness to have had their lot of Life in some notable Conjunctures of Ages past; but the uncertainty of future Times hath tempted few to make a part in Ages to come. And surely, he that hath taken the true Altitude of Things, and rightly calculated the degenerate state of this Age, is not like to envy those that shall live in the next, much less three or four hundred Years hence, when no Man can comfortably imagine what Face this World will carry: and therefore since every Age makes a step unto the end of all things, and the Scripture affords so hard a Character of the last Times; quiet Minds will be content with their Generations, and rather bless Ages past than be ambitious of those to come.

Tho Age had set no Seal upon his Face, yet a dim Eye might clearly discover Fifty in his Actions; and therefore since Wisdom is the gray Hair, and an unspotted Life old Age; altho his Years came short, he might have been said to have held up with longer Livers, and to have been Solomon's Old Man.[39] And surely if we deduct all those days of our Life which we might wish unlived, and which abate the comfort of those we now live; if we reckon up only those days which God hath accepted of our Lives, a Life of good Years will hardly be a span long: the Son in this sense may out-live the Father, and none be climacterically old. He that early arriveth unto the Parts and Prudence of Age, is happily old without the uncomfortable Attendants of it; and 'tis superfluous to live unto gray Hairs, when in a precocious Temper we anticipate the Virtues of them. In brief, he cannot be accounted young who out-liveth the old Man. He that hath early arrived unto the measure of a perfect Stature in Christ, hath already fulfilled the prime and longest Intention of his Being: and one day lived after the perfect Rule of Piety, is to be preferred before sinning Immortality.

Although he attained not unto the Years of his Predecessors, yet he wanted not those preserving Virtues which confirm the thread of weaker Constitutions. Cautelous Chastity and crafty Sobriety were far from him; those Jewels were Paragon, without Flaw, Hair, Ice, or Cloud in him: which affords me an hint to proceed in these good Wishes and few *Memento's* unto you.

Tread softly and circumspectly in this funambulous Track and narrow Path of Goodness: pursue Virtue virtuously; be sober and temperate, not to preserve your Body in a sufficiency to wanton Ends; not to spare your Purse; not to be free from the Infamy of common Transgressors that way, and thereby to ballance or palliate obscure and closer Vices; nor simply to enjoy Health: by all which you may leaven good Actions, and render Virtues disputable; but in one Word, that you may truly serve God; which every Sickness will tell you, you cannot well do without Health. The sick mans Sacrifice is but a lame Oblation. Pious

Treasures laid up in healthful days, excuse the defect of sick Non-performances; without which we must needs look back with Anxiety upon the lost opportunities of Health; and may have cause rather to envy than pity the Ends of penitent Malefactors, who go with clear parts unto the last Act of their Lives; and in the integrity of their Faculties return their Spirit unto God that gave it.

Consider whereabout thou art in *Cebes* his Table, or that old philosophical Pinax of the Life of Man; whether thou art still in the Road of Uncertainties; whether thou hast yet entred the narrow Gate, got up the Hill and asperous way which leadeth unto the House of Sanity, or taken that purifying Potion from the hand of sincere Erudition, which may send thee clear and pure a way unto a virtuous and happy Life.

In this virtuous Voyage let not disappointment cause Despondency, nor difficulty Despair; think not that you are sailing from Lima to Manillia, [40] wherein thou may'st tye up the Rudder, and sleep before the Wind; but expect rough Seas, Flaws, and contrary Blasts; and 'tis well if by many cross Tacks and Verings thou arrivest at thy Port. Sit not down in the popular Seats and common Level of Virtues, but endeavour to make them Heroical. Offer not only Peace-Offerings but Holocausts unto God. To serve him singly, to serve our selves, were too partial a piece of Piety, nor likely to place us in the highest Mansions of Glory.

He that is chaste and continent, not to impair his Strength, or terrified by Contagion, will hardly be heroically virtuous. Adjourn not that Virtue unto those Years when Cato could lend out his Wife, and impotent *Satyrs* write Satyrs against Lust: but be chaste in thy flaming days, when Alexander dared not trust his Eyes upon the fair Daughters of Darius, and when so many Men think there is no other way but Origen's.[41]

Be charitable before Wealth makes thee covetous, and lose not the Glory of the Mite. If Riches increase, let thy Mind hold pace with them; and think it not enough to be liberal, but munificent. Tho a Cup of cold Water from some hand may not be without its Reward; yet stick not thou for Wine and Oyl for the Wounds of the distressed: and treat the Poor as our Saviour did the Multitude, to the Relicks of some Baskets.

Trust not to the Omnipotency of Gold, or say unto it, Thou art my Confidence: Kiss not thy Hand when thou beholdest that terrestrial Sun, nor bore thy Ear unto its Servitude. A Slave unto Mammon makes no Servant unto God: Covetousness cracks the Sinews of Faith, numbs the Apprehension of any thing above Sense, and only affected with the certainty of things present, makes a peradventure of Things to come; lives but unto one World, nor hopes but fears another; makes our own Death sweet unto others, bitter unto our selves; gives a dry Funeral, Scenical Mourning, and no wet Eyes at the Grave.

If Avarice be thy Vice, yet make it not thy Punishment: miserable Men commiserate not themselves, bowelless unto themselves, and merciless unto their own Bowels. Let the fruition of Things bless the possession of them, and take no satisfaction in dying but living rich: for since thy good Works, not thy Goods, will follow thee; since Riches are an Appurtenance of Life, and no dead Man is rich, to famish in Plenty, and live poorly to dye rich, were a multiplying improvement in Madness, and Use upon Use in Folly.

Persons lightly dip'd, not grain'd in generous Honesty, are but pale in Goodness, and faint hued in Sincerity: but be thou what thou virtuously art, and let not the Ocean wash away thy Tincture: stand magnetically upon that Axis where prudent Simplicity hath fix'd thee, and let no Temptation invert the Poles of thy Honesty: and that Vice may be uneasie, and even monstrous unto thee, let iterated good Acts, and long confirmed Habits, make Vertue natural, or a second Nature in thee. And since few or none prove eminently vertuous but from some advantageous Foundations in their Temper and natural Inclinations; study thy self betimes, and early find, what Nature bids thee to be, or tells thee what thou may'st be. They who thus timely descend into themselves, cultivating the good Seeds which Nature hath set in them, and improving their prevalent Inclinations to Perfection, become not Shrubs, but Cedars in their Generation; and to be in the form of the best of the Bad, or the worst of the Good, will be no satisfaction unto them.

Let not the Law of thy Country be the non ultra of thy Honesty, nor think that always good enough which the Law will make good. Narrow not the Law of Charity, Equity, Mercy; joyn Gospel Righteousness with Legal Right; be not a meer Gamaliel in the Faith; but let the Sermon in the Mount be thy *Targum* unto the Law of Sinai.

Make not the Consequences of Vertue the Ends thereof: be not beneficent for a Name or Cymbal of Applause, nor exact and punctual in Commerce, for the Advantages of Trust and Credit, which attend the Reputation of just and true Dealing; for such Rewards, tho unsought for, plain Virtue will bring with her, whom all Men honour, tho they pursue not. To have other bye Ends in good Actions, sowers laudable Performances, which must have deeper Roots, Motions, and Instigations, to give them the Stamp of Vertues.

Tho humane Infirmity may betray thy heedless days into the popular ways of Extravagancy, yet let not thine own depravity, or the torrent of vicious Times, carry thee into desperate Enormities in Opinions, Manners, or Actions: if thou hast dip'd thy foot in the River, yet venture not over Rubicon; run not into Extremities from whence there is no Regression, nor be ever so closely shut up within the holds of Vice and Iniquity, as not to find some Escape by a Postern of Resipiscency.

Owe not thy Humility unto Humiliation by Adversity, but look humbly down in that State when others look upward upon thee: be patient in the Age of Pride and days of Will and Impatiency, when Men live but by Intervals of Reason, under the Sovereignty of Humor and Passion, when 'tis in the Power of every one to transform thee out of thy self, and put thee into the short Madness. If you cannot imitate Job, yet come not short of Socrates,[42] and those patient Pagans, who tired the Tongues of their Enemies, while they perceiv'd they spet their Malice at Brazen Walls and Statues.

Let Age, not Envy, draw Wrinkles on thy Cheeks: be content to be envied, but envy not, Emulation may be plausible, and Indignation allowable; but admit no Treaty with that Passion which no Circumstance can make good. A Displacency at the good of others, because they enjoy it, altho we do not want it, is an absurd Depravity, sticking fast unto humane Nature from its primitive Corruption; which he that can well subdue, were a Christian of the first Magnitude, and for ought I know, may have one foot already in Heaven.

While thou so hotly disclaimst the Devil, be not guilty of Diabolism; fall not in to one Name with that unclean Spirit, nor act his Nature whom thou so much abhorrest; that is, to accuse, calumniate, backbite, whisper, detract, or sinistrously interpret others; degenerous Depravities and narrow-minded Vices, not only below S. Paul's noble Christian, but Aristotle's true Gentleman.[43] Trust not with some, that the Epistle of S. James is Apocryphal, and so read with less fear that stabbing truth, that in company with this Vice thy Religion is in vain. Moses broke the Tables without breaking of the Law; but where Charity is broke the Law it self is shattered, which cannot be whole without Love, that is the fulfilling of it. Look humbly upon thy Virtues, and tho thou art rich in some, yet think thy self poor and naked without that crowning Grace, which thinketh no Evil, which envieth not, which beareth, believeth, hopeth, endureth all things. With these sure Graces, while busie Tongues are crying out for a drop of cold Water, Mutes may be in Happiness, and sing the *Trisagium*[44] in Heaven.

Let not the Sun in Capricorn go down upon thy Wrath, but write thy Wrongs in Water; draw the Curtain of Night upon Injuries; shut them up in the Tower of Oblivion,[45] and let them be as tho they had not been. Forgive thine Enemies totally, and without any Reserve of hope, that however, God will revenge thee.

Be substantially great in thy self, and more than thou appearest unto others; and let the World be deceived in thee, as they are in the Lights of Heaven. Hang early Plummets upon the Heels of Pride, and let Ambition have but an Epicycle or narrow circuit in thee. Measure not thy self by thy Morning shadow, but by the Extent of thy Grave; and reckon thy self above the Earth by the Line thou must be contented with under it. Spread not into boundless Expansions either of Designs or Desires. Think not that Mankind liveth but for a few, and that the rest are born but to serve the Ambition of those, who make but Flies of Men, and Wildernesses of whole Nations. Swell not into Actions which embroil and confound the Earth; but be one of those violent ones which *force the Kingdom of Heaven*.[46] If thou must needs reign, be Zeno's King, and enjoy that Empire which every Man gives himself. Certainly the iterated Injunctions of Christ unto Humility, Meekness, Patience, and that despised Train of Virtues, cannot but make pathetical Impressions upon those who have well considered the Affairs of all Ages, wherein Pride, Ambition, and Vain-glory, have led up the worst of Actions, and whereunto Confusion, Tragedies, and Acts denying all Religion, do owe their Originals.

Rest not in an Ovation,[47] but a Triumph over thy Passions; chain up the unruly Legion of thy Breast; behold thy Trophies within thee, not without thee: Lead thine own Captivity captive, and be Cæsar unto thy self.

Give no quarter unto those Vices which are of thine inward Family; and having a Root in thy Temper, plead a Right and Propriety in thee. Examine well thy complexional Inclinations. Raise early Batteries against those strong-holds built upon the Rock of Nature, and make this a great part of the Militia of thy Life. The politick Nature of Vice must be opposed by Policy, and therefore wiser Honesties Project and plot against Sin; wherein notwithstanding we are not to rest in Generals, or the trite Stratagems of Art: that may succeed with one Temper which may prove successless with another. There is no Community or Commonwealth of Virtue; every Man must study his own Œconomy, and erect these Rules unto the Figure of himself.

Lastly, If length of Days be thy Portion, make it not thy Expectation: reckon not upon long Life, but live always beyond thy Account. He that so often surviveth his Expectation, lives many Lives, and will hardly complain of the shortness of his Days. Time past is gone like a shadow; make Times to come, present; conceive that near which may be far off; approximate thy last Times by present Apprehensions of them: live like a Neighbour unto Death, and think there is but little to come. And since there is something in us that must still live on, joyn both Lives together; unite them in thy Thoughts and Actions, and live in one but for the other. He who thus ordereth the Purposes of this Life, will never be far from the next; and is in some manner already in it, by an happy Conformity, and close Apprehension of it.

F I N I S.

NOTES

1. Cum mors venerit, in medio Tibure Sardinia est. [Martial Epig. iv.60.5]

2. In the King's Forest they set the Figure of a broad Arrow upon Trees that are to be cut down.

3 Hippoc. Epidem.

4. Antipodes. Bellonius de Avibus.

5. Monstra contingunt in medicina Hippoc. Strange and rare Escapes there happen sometimes in Physick.

6. Angeli Victorii Consultationes.

7. Matth. iv. 25.

8. Aristoteles nullum animal nisi oestu recedente expirare affirmat: observatum id multum in Gallico Oceano & duntaxat in Homine compertum, lib. 2. cap. 101. [Pliny NH ii.220;]

9. Auris pars pendula Lobus dicitur, non omnibus ea pars est auribus; non enim üs qui noctu nati sunt, sed qui interdiu, maxima ex parte. Com. in Aristot. de Animal. lib. I.

10. According to the Egyptian Hieroglyphick.

11. Turkish History.

12 Probably from *boufée,* inflation.

13. In the Poet Dante his description.

14. (at sexta cervice) i.e., by six persons

15. De morbis Puerorum.

16. Morta, the Deity of Death or Fate.

17. When Mens Faces are drawn with resemblance to some other Animals, the Italians call it, to be drawn in Caricatura.

18. Ulmus de usu barbæ humanæ.

19. The Life of a man is Threescore and Ten. [Or fourscore, for the strong; Psalm 90:10.]

20. See Picotus de Rheumatismo. Seemingly an error, as Picotus does not discuss this affliction. See "Sir Thomas Browne and the Disease called the Morgellons" for a discussion of the disease.

21. MS. Sloan 1862, in Wilkin, continues:
Though hairs afford but fallible conjectures, yet we cannot but take notice of them. They grow not equally on bodies after death: women's skulls afford moss as well as men's, and the best I have seen was upon a woman's skull, taken up and laid in a room after twenty-five years' burial. Though the skin be made the place of hairs, yet sometimes they are found on the heart and inward parts. The plica or gluey locks happen unto both sexes, and being cut off will come again: but they are wary of cutting off the same, for fear of headache and other diseases.

22. His upper and lower Jaw being solid, and without distinct rows of Teeth.

23. Twice tell over his Teeth never live to threescore Years.

24. In the MS. Sloan 1862 occurs the following paragraph:
Affection had so blinded some of his nearest relations, as to retain some hope of a postliminious life, and that he might come to life again, and therefore would not have him coffined before the third day. Some such virbiasses [so in MS.] I confess we find in story, and one or two I remember myself, but they lived not long after. Some contingent re-animations are to be hoped in diseases wherein the lamp of life is but puffed out and seemingly choaked, and not where the oil is quite spent and exhausted. Though Nonnes will have it a fever, yet of what disease Lazarus first died, it is uncertain from the text, as his second death from good authentic history; but since some persons conceived to be dead do sometimes return again unto evidence of life, that miracle was wisely managed by our Saviour; for had he not been dead four days and under corruption, there had not wanted enough who would have cavilled the same, which the scripture now puts out of doubt; and tradition also confirmeth, that he lived thirty years after, and being pursued by the Jews, came by sea into Provence, by Marseilles, with Mary Magdalen, Maximinus, and others: where remarkable places carry their names unto this day. But to arise from the grave to return again into it, is but an uncomfortable reviction. Few men would be content to cradle it once again: except a man can lead his second life better than the first, a man may be double condemned for living evilly twice, which were but to make the second death in scripture the third, and to accumulate in the punishment of two bad livers at the last day. To have performed the duty of corruption in the grave, to live again as far form sin as death, and arise like our Saviour for ever, are the only satisfactions of well-weighed expectations.

25. Ἀσφαλέστατος καὶ ῥήϊστος, seucrissima & facillimæ Hippocrat.

26. Pro febre quartana raro sonat campana. (quartan ague rarely sounds the [death]bell).

27. The caul or omentum; lining of the stomach and intestines.

28. 'Sir A. J.' - Sir Arthur Jenny.

29. Cardan in his Encomium Podagræ reckoneth this among the Dona Podagræ, that they are delivered thereby from the Pthysis and Stone in the Bladder.

30. Hippoc. de Insomniis.

31. Tabes maxime contingunt ab anno decimo octavo ad trigesimum quintum, Hippoc. [in the Aphorisms, V, 9.]

32. A sound Child cut out of the Body of the Mother.

33.Natos ad flumina primum deferimus saeuoque gelu duramus et undis. [Virgil Æneid IX.603-604.

34. Or, like an auction – candles were used as a timer to end the bidding.

35. Julii Cæsaris Scaligeri quod fuit. Joseph Scaliger in vita patris.

36. Summum nec metuas diem nec optes. [Martial, Epigrams x.lxvii]

37. Who upon some Accounts, and Traditions, is said to have lived 30 Years after he

was raised by our Saviour. Baronius. (Cardinal Cesare Baronio, 1538-1607)

38. In the Speech of Vulteius in Lucan, animating his Souldiers in a great struggle to kill one another. Decernite Lethum & metus omnis abest, cupias quodcunq; necesse est. All fear is over do but resolve to dye, and make your Desires meet Necessity. [Lucan IV.486-487.]

39. Wisdom cap. iv.

40. Through the Pacifick Sea, with a constant Gale from the East.

41. Who is said to have castrated himself.

42. Ira furor brevis est.

43. See Arist. Ethicks Chapt. of Magnaminity.

44. Holy, Holy, Holy.

45. Even when the Days are shortest; alluding to the Tower of *Oblivion*, mentioned by *Procopius,* which was the name of a Tower of Imprisonment among the *Persians:* whosoever was put thereinhe was as it were buried alive, and it was Death for any but to name it

46. Matthew xi.

47. Ovation, a petty and minor kind of Triumph.

HYDRIOTAPHIA:
URN BURIAL

or, a discourse of the
sepulchral urns
lately found in Norfolk

EN SUM, QUOD DIGITIS QUINQUE LEGATOR, ONUS –
PROPERTIUS SEXTUS. ELEGIAE 4.

(Look, I am become a burden which five fingers may lift)

EPISTLE DEDICATORY

TO MY WORTHY AND HONOURED FRIEND,
THOMAS LE GROS, OF CROSTWICK, ESQUIRE.

When the funeral pyre was out, and the last valediction over, men took a lasting adieu of their interred friends, little expecting the curiosity of future ages should comment upon their ashes; and, having no old experience of the duration of their relicks, held no opinion of such after-considerations.

But who knows the fate of his bones, or how often he is to be buried? Who hath the oracle of his ashes, or whither they are to be scattered? The relicks of many lie like the ruins of Pompey's,[1] in all parts of the earth; and when they arrive at your hands these may seem to have wandered far, who, in a direct and meridian travel,[2] have but few miles of known earth between yourself and the pole.

That the bones of Theseus should be seen again in Athens[3] was not beyond conjecture and hopeful expectation: but that these should arise so opportunely to serve yourself was an hit of fate, and honour beyond prediction. We cannot but wish these urns might have the effect of theatrical vessels and great Hippodrome urns[4] in Rome, to resound the acclamations and honour due unto you. But these are sad and sepulchral pitchers, which have no joyful voices; silently expressing old mortality, the ruins of forgotten times, and can only speak with life, how long in this corruptible frame some parts may be uncorrupted; yet able to outlast bones long unborn, and noblest pile among us.

We present not these as any strange sight or spectacle unknown to your eyes, who have beheld the best of urns and noblest variety of ashes; who are yourself no slender master of antiquities, and can daily command the view of so many imperial faces; which raiseth your thoughts unto old things and consideration of times before you, when even living men were antiquities; when the living might exceed the dead, and to depart this world could not be properly said to go unto the greater number.[5] And so run up your thoughts upon the ancient of days, the antiquary's truest object, unto whom the eldest parcels are young, and earth itself an infant, and without Egyptian[6] account makes but small noise in thousands.

We were hinted by the occasion, not catched the opportunity to write of old things, or intrude upon the antiquary. We are coldly drawn unto discourses of antiquities, who have scarce time before us to comprehend new things, or make

---

1. "Pompeios juvenes Asia atque Europa, sed ipsum terra tegit Libyos."
2. Little directly but sea, between your house and Greenland.
3. Brought back by Cimon Plutarch.
4. The great urns at the Hippodrome at Rome, conceived to resound the voices of people at their shows.
5. "Abiit ad plures."
6. Which makes the world so many years old.

out learned novelties. But seeing they arose, as they lay almost in silence among us, at least in short account suddenly passed over, we were very unwilling they should die again, and be buried twice among us.

Beside, to preserve the living, and make the dead to live, to keep men out of their urns, and discourse of human fragments in them, is not impertinent unto our profession; whose study is life and death, who daily behold examples of mortality, and of all men least need artificial mementos, or coffins by our bedside, to mind us of our graves.

'Tis time to observe occurrences, and let nothing remarkable escape us: the supinity of elder days hath left so much in silence, or time hath so martyred the records, that the most industrious heads do find no easy work to erect a new Britannia.

'Tis opportune to look back upon old times, and contemplate our forefathers. Great examples grow thin, and to be fetched from the passed world. Simplicity flies away, and iniquity comes at long strides upon us. We have enough to do to make up ourselves from present and passed times, and the whole stage of things scarce serveth for our instruction. A complete piece of virtue must be made from the Centos of all ages, as all the beauties of Greece could make but one handsome Venus.

When the bones of King Arthur were digged up,[7] the old race might think they beheld therein some originals of themselves; unto these of our urns none here can pretend relation, and can only behold the relicks of those persons who, in their life giving the laws unto their predecessors, after long obscurity, now lie at their mercies. But, remembering the early civility they brought upon these countries, and forgetting long-passed mischiefs, we mercifully preserve their bones, and piss not upon their ashes.

In the offer of these antiquities we drive not at ancient families, so long outlasted by them. We are far from erecting your worth upon the pillars of your forefathers, whose merits you illustrate. We honour your old virtues, conformable unto times before you, which are the noblest armoury. And, having long experience of your friendly conversation, void of empty formality, full of freedom, constant and generous honesty, I look upon you as a gem of the old rock,[8] and must profess myself even to urn and ashes. – Your ever faithful Friend and Servant,

Thomas Browne.
Norwich, May 1st.

7. *In the time of Henry the Second.*
8. *"Adamas de rupe veteri praestantissimus."*

CHAPTER I

In the deep discovery of the subterranean world a shallow part would satisfy some inquirers; who, if two or three yards were open about the surface, would not care to rake the bowels of *Potosi*,[1] and regions toward the centre. Nature hath furnished one part of the earth, and man another. The treasures of time lie high, in urns, coins, and monuments, scarce below the roots of some vegetables. Time hath endless rarities, and shows of all varieties; which reveals old things in heaven, makes new discoveries in earth, and even earth itself a discovery. That great antiquity America lay buried for thousands of years, and a large part of the earth is still in the urn unto us.

Though if Adam were made out of an extract of the earth, all parts might challenge a restitution, yet few have returned their bones far lower than they might receive them; not affecting the graves of giants, under hilly and heavy coverings, but content with less than their own depth, have wished their bones might lie soft, and the earth be light upon them. Even such as hope to rise again, would not be content with central interment, or so desperately to place their relicks as to lie beyond discovery; and in no way to be seen again; which happy contrivance hath made communication with our forefathers, and left unto our view some parts, which they never beheld themselves.

Though earth hath engrossed the name, yet water hath proved the smartest grave; which in forty days swallowed almost mankind, and the living creation; fishes not wholly escaping, except the salt ocean were handsomely contempered by a mixture of the fresh element.

Many have taken voluminous pains to determine the state of the soul upon disunion; but men have been most phantastical in the singular contrivances of their corporal dissolution: whilst the soberest nations have rested in two ways, of simple inhumation and burning.

That carnal interment or burying was of the elder date, the old examples of Abraham and the patriarchs are sufficient to illustrate; and were without competition, if it could be made out that Adam was buried near Damascus, or Mount Calvary, according to some tradition. God himself, that buried but one, was pleased to make choice of this way, collectible from Scripture expression, and the hot contest between Satan and the archangel about discovering the body of Moses. But the practice of burning was also of great antiquity, and of no slender extent. For (not to derive the same from Hercules) noble descriptions there are hereof in the Grecian funerals of Homer, in the formal obsequies of Patroclus and Achilles; and somewhat elder in the Theban war, and solemn combustion of

---

1. *The rich mountain of Peru (silver ore).*

Meneceus, and Archemorus, contemporary unto Jair the eighth judge of Israel. Confirmable also among the Trojans, from the funeral pyre of Hector, burnt before the gates of Troy: and the burning of Penthesilea the Amazonian queen[2]: and long continuance of that practice, in the inward countries of Asia; while as low as the reign of Julian, we find that the king of Chionia[3] burnt the body of his son, and interred the ashes in a silver urn.

The same practice extended also far west[4]; and besides Herulians, Getes, and Thracians, was in use with most of the Celtae, Sarmatians, Germans, Gauls, Danes, Swedes, Norwegians; not to omit some use thereof among Carthaginians and Americans. Of greater antiquity among the Romans than most opinion, or Pliny seems to allow: for (besides the old table laws[5] of burning or burying within the city, of making the funeral fire with planed wood, or quenching the fire with wine), Manlius the consul burnt the body of his son: Numa, by special clause of his will, was not burnt but buried; and Remus was solemnly burned, according to the description of Ovid.[6]

Cornelius Sylla was not the first whose body was burned in Rome, but the first of the Cornelian family; which being indifferently, not frequently used before; from that time spread, and became the prevalent practice. Not totally pursued in the highest run of cremation; for when even crows were funerally burnt, Poppaea the wife of Nero found a peculiar grave interment. Now as all customs were founded upon some bottom of reason, so there wanted not grounds for this; according to several apprehensions of the most rational dissolution. Some being of the opinion of Thales, that water was the original of all things, thought it most equal to submit unto the principle of putrefaction, and conclude in a moist relentment [i.e., dissolution]. Others conceived it most natural to end in fire, as due unto the master principle in the composition, according to the doctrine of Heraclitus; and therefore heaped up large piles, more actively to waft them toward that element, whereby they also declined a visible degeneration into worms, and left a lasting parcel of their composition.

Some apprehended a purifying virtue in fire, refining the grosser commixture, and firing out the aethereal particles so deeply immersed in it. And such as by tradition or rational conjecture held any hint of the final pyre of all things; or that this element at last must be too hard for all the rest; might conceive most naturally of the fiery dissolution. Others pretending no natural grounds, politickly declined the malice of enemies upon their buried bodies. Which consideration led Sylla unto this practice; who having thus served the body of Marius, could

---

2. *Q. Calaber. lib. i*

3. *Gumbrates, king of Chionia, a country near Persia.*

4. *Arnold. not. in Caes. COmm. L. Gyraldus. Kirkmannus.*

5. *XII. Tabulae, pt i., de jure sacro, 'Hominem mortuum in urbe ne sepelito neve urito.'*

6. *"Ultimo prolata subdita flamma rogo," &c. Ovid Fast., lib. iv., 856.*

not but fear a retaliation upon his own; entertained after in the civil wars, and revengeful contentions of Rome.

But as many nations embraced, and many left it indifferent, so others too much affected, or strictly declined this practice. The Indian *Brachmans* seemed too great friends unto fire, who burnt themselves alive and thought it the noblest way to end their days in fire; according to the expression of the Indian, burning himself at Athens, in his last words upon the pyre unto the amazed spectators, *"thus I make myself immortal."*[1]

But the Chaldeans, the great idolaters of fire, abhorred the burning of their carcases, as a pollution of that deity. The Persian magi declined it upon the like scruples, and being only solicitous about their bones, exposed their flesh to the prey of birds and dogs. And the Persees now in India, which expose their bodies unto vultures, and endure not so much as *feretra* or biers of wood, the proper fuel of fire, are led on with such niceties. But whether the ancient Germans, who burned their dead, held any such fear to pollute their deity of *Herthu*s, or the earth, we have no authentic conjecture.

The Egyptians were afraid of fire, not as a deity, but a devouring element, mercilessly consuming their bodies, and leaving too little of them; and therefore by precious embalmments, depositure in dry earths, or handsome inclosure in glasses, contrived the notablest ways of integral conservation. And from such Egyptian scruples, imbibed by Pythagoras, it may be conjectured that Numa and the Pythagorical sect first waived the fiery solution.

The Scythians, who swore by wind and sword, that is, by life and death, were so far from burning their bodies, that they declined all interment, and made their graves in the air: and the *Ichthyophagi*, or fish-eating nations about Egypt, affected the sea for their grave; thereby declining visible corruption, and restoring the debt of their bodies. Whereas the old heroes, in Homer, dreaded nothing more than water or drowning; probably upon the old opinion of the fiery substance of the soul, only extinguishable by that element; and therefore the poet emphatically implieth[2] the total destruction in this kind of death, which happened to Ajax Oileus.

The old Balearians[3] had a peculiar mode, for they used great urns and much wood, but no fire in their burials, while they bruised the flesh and bones of the dead, crowded them into urns, and laid heaps of wood upon them. And the *Chinois*[4] without cremation or urnal interment of their bodies, make use of trees and much burning, while they plant a pine-tree by their grave, and burn great numbers of printed draughts of slaves and horses over it, civilly content with their companies *in effigy*, which barbarous nations exact unto reality.

---

1. *And therefore the inscription on his tomb was made accordingly, "Hic Damase."*
2. *Which Magius reads* ἐξαπόλωλε.
3. *Diodorus Siculus*
4. *Ramusius in Navigat.*

Christians abhorred this way of obsequies, and though they sticked not to give their bodies to be burnt in their lives, detested that mode after death: affecting rather a depositure than absumption, and properly submitting unto the sentence of God, to return not unto ashes but unto dust again, and conformable unto the practice of the patriarchs, the interment of our Saviour, of Peter, Paul, and the ancient martyrs. And so far at last declining promiscuous interment with Pagans, that some have suffered ecclesiastical censures,[1] for making no scruple thereof.

The Mussulman believers will never admit this fiery resolution. For they hold a present trial from their black and white angels in the grave; which they must have made so hollow, that they may rise upon their knees.

The Jewish nation, though they entertained the old way of inhumation, yet sometimes admitted this practice. For the men of Jabesh burnt the body of Saul; and by no prohibited practice, to avoid contagion or pollution, in time of pestilence, burnt the bodies of their friends.[2] And when they burnt not their dead bodies, yet sometimes used great burnings near and about them, deducible from the expressions concerning Jehoram, Zedechias, and the sumptuous pyre of Asa. And were so little averse from Pagan burning, that the Jews lamenting the death of Caesar their friend, and revenger on Pompey, frequented the place where his body was burnt for many nights together.[3] And as they raised noble monuments and mausoleums for their own nation,[4] so they were not scrupulous in erecting some for others, according to the practice of Daniel, who left that lasting sepulchral pile in *Ecbatana*, for the Median and Persian kings.[5]

But even in times of subjection and hottest use, they conformed not unto the Roman practice of burning; whereby the prophecy was secured concerning the body of Christ, that it should not see corruption, or a bone should not be broken; which we believe was also providentially prevented, from the soldier's spear and nails that passed by the little bones both in his hands and feet; not of ordinary contrivance, that it should not corrupt on the cross, according to the laws of Roman crucifixion, or an hair of his head perish, though observable in Jewish customs, to cut the hair of malefactors.

Nor in their long cohabitation with Egyptians, crept into a custom of their exact embalming, wherein deeply slashing the muscles, and taking out the brains and entrails, they had broken the subject of so entire a resurrection, nor fully answered the types of Enoch, Elijah, or Jonah, which yet to prevent or restore, was of equal facility unto that rising power able to break the fasciations and bands of death, to get clear out of the cerecloth, and an hundred pounds of ointment, and out of the sepulchre before the stone was rolled from it.

---

1. *Martialis the Bishop.*   2. *Amos vi. 10.*

3.*Suetonius, in Vita Julius Caesar*

4. *As in that magnificent sepulchral monument erected by Simon. – 1 Macc. xiii.*

5. *Κατασκεύασμα θαθμασίως πεποιλημένον, whereof a Jewish priest had always custody unto Josephus his days. – Jos. Antiq., lib. x.*

But though they embraced not this practice of burning, yet entertained they many ceremonies agreeable unto Greek and Roman obsequies. And he that observeth their funeral feasts, their lamentations at the grave, their music, and weeping mourners; how they closed the eyes of their friends, how they washed, anointed, and kissed the dead; may easily conclude these were not mere Pagan civilities. But whether that mournful burthen, and treble calling out after Absalom,[1] had any reference unto the last conclamation, and triple valediction, used by other nations, we hold but a wavering conjecture.

Civilians make sepulture but of the law of nations, others do naturally found it and discover it also in animals. They that are so thick-skinned as still to credit the story of the *Phoenix*, may say something for animal burning. More serious conjectures find some examples of sepulture in elephants, cranes, the sepulchral cells of pismires, and practice of bees – which civil society carrieth out their dead, and hath exequies, if not interments.

---

1. 2 Sam. XVIII. 33

Chapter II

The solemnities, ceremonies, rites of their cremation or interment, so solemnly delivered by authors, we shall not disparage our reader to repeat. Only the last and lasting part in their urns, collected bones and ashes, we cannot wholly omit or decline that subject, which occasion lately presented, in some discovered among us.

In a field of Old Walsingham, not many months past, were digged up between forty and fifty urns, deposited in a dry and sandy soil, not a yard deep, nor far from one another. – Not all strictly of one figure, but most answering these described; some containing two pounds of bones, and teeth, with fresh impressions of their combustion; besides the extraneous substances, like pieces of small boxes, or combs handsomely wrought, handles of small brass instruments, brazen nippers, and in one some kind of opal.

Near the same plot of ground, for about six yards compass, were digged up coals and incinerated substances, which begat conjecture that this was the *ustrina* or place of burning their bodies, or some sacrificing place unto the *Manes*, which was properly below the surface of the ground, as the arae and altars unto the gods and heroes above it.

That these were the urns of Romans from the common custom and place where they were found, is no obscure conjecture, not far from a Roman garrison, and but five miles from Brancaster, set down by ancient record under the name of *Brannodunum*. And where the adjoining town, containing seven parishes, in no very different sound, but Saxon termination, still retains the name of Burnham, which being an early station, it is not improbable the neighbour parts were filled with habitations, either of Romans themselves, or Britons Romanized, which observed the Roman customs.

Nor is it improbable, that the Romans early possessed this country. For though we meet not with such strict particulars of these parts before the new institution of Constantine and military charge of the count of the Saxon shore, and that about the Saxon invasions, the Dalmatian horsemen were in the garrison of Brancaster; yet in the time of Claudius, Vespasian, and Severus, we find no less than three legions dispersed through the province of Britain. And as high as the reign of Claudius a great overthrow was given unto the Iceni, by the Roman lieutenant Ostorius. Not long after, the country was so molested, that, in hope of a better state, Prastaagus bequeathed his kingdom unto Nero and his daughters; and Boadicea, his queen, fought the last decisive battle with Paulinus. After which time, and conquest of Agricola, the lieutenant of Vespasian, probable it is,

---

1. *In one sent me by my worthy friend, Dr. Thomas Witherly of Walsingham*

they wholly possessed this country; ordering it into garrisons or habitations best suitable with their securities. And so some Roman habitations not improbable in these parts, as high as the time of Vespasian, where the Saxons after seated, in whose thin-filled maps we yet find the name of Walsingham. Now if the Iceni were but Gammadims, Anconians, or men that lived in an angle, wedge, or elbow of Britain, according to the original etymology, this country will challenge the emphatical appellation, as most properly making the elbow or *iken* of Icenia.[1]

That Britain was notably populous is undeniable, from that expression of Caesar.[2] That the Romans themselves were early in no small numbers – seventy thousand, with their associates, slain, by Boadicea, affords a sure account. And though not many Roman habitations are now known, yet some, by old works, rampiers, coins, and urns, do testify their possessions. Some urns have been found at Castor, some also about Southcreak, and, not many years past, no less than ten in a field at Buston, not near any recorded garrison. Nor is it strange to find Roman coins of copper and silver among us; of Vespasian, Trajan, Adrian, Commodus, Antoninus, Severus, &c.; but the greater number of Dioclesian, Constantine, Constans, Valens, with many of Victorinus Posthumius, Tetricus, and the thirty tyrants in the reign of Gallienus; and some as high as Adrianus have been found about Thetford, or Sitomagus, mentioned in the *Itinerary* of Antoninus, as the way from Venta or Castor unto London. But the most frequent discovery is made at the two Castors by Norwich and Yarmouth at Burghcastle, and Brancaster.

Besides the Norman, Saxon, and Danish pieces of Cuthred, Canutus, William, Matilda, and others, some British coins of gold have been dispersedly found, and no small number of silver pieces near Norwich, with a rude head upon the obverse, and an ill-formed horse on the reverse, with inscriptions *Ic. Duro. T.*; whether implying Iceni, Durotriges, Tascia, or Trinobantes, we leave to higher conjecture. Vulgar chronology will have Norwich Castle as old as Julius Caesar; but his distance from these parts, and its Gothick form of structure, abridgeth such antiquity. The British coins afford conjecture of early habitation in these parts, though the city of Norwich arose from the ruins of Venta; and though, perhaps, not without some habitation before, was enlarged, builded, and nominated by the Saxons. In what bulk or populosity it stood in the old East-Angle monarchy, tradition and history are silent. Considerable it was in the Danish eruptions, when Sueno burnt Thetford and Norwich, and *Ulfketel*, the governor thereof, was able to make some resistance, and after endeavoured to burn the Danish navy.

---

1. *Unfortunately, iken does not signify an elbow; and it appears the Iceni derive their name from river Ouse, on whose banks they resided - anciently called Iken, Yken, or Ycin. Whence also, Ikenild-street, Ikenthorpe, Ikenworth.*
2. *"Hominum infinita multitudo est creberrimaque; aedificia fere Gallicis consimilia."– Caesar de Bello. Gal., lib. v.*

How the Romans left so many coins in countries of their conquests seems of hard resolution; except we consider how they buried them under ground when, upon barbarous invasions, they were fain to desert their habitations in most part of their empire, and the strictness of their laws forbidding to transfer them to any other uses: wherein the Spartans[1] were singular, who, to make their copper money useless, contempered it with vinegar. That the Britons left any, some wonder, since their money was iron and iron rings before Caesar; and those of after-stamp by permission, and but small in bulk and bigness. That so few of the Saxons remain, because, overcome by succeeding conquerors upon the place, their coins, by degrees, passed into other stamps and the marks of after-ages.

Than the time of these urns deposited, or precise antiquity of these relicks, nothing of more uncertainty; for since the lieutenant of Claudius seems to have made the first progress into these parts, since Boadicea was overthrown by the forces of Nero, and Agricola put a full end to these conquests, it is not probable the country was fully garrisoned or planted before; and, therefore, however these urns might be of later date, not likely of higher antiquity.

And the succeeding emperors desisted not from their conquests in these and other parts, as testified by history and medal-inscription yet extant: the province of Britain, in so divided a distance from Rome, beholding the faces of many imperial persons, and in large account; no fewer than Caesar, Claudius, Britannicus, Vespasian, Titus, Adrian, Severus, Commodus, Geta, and Caracalla.

A great obscurity herein, because no medal or emperor's coin enclosed, which might denote the date of their interments; observable in many urns, and found in those of Spitalfields, by London,[2] which contained the coins of Claudius, Vespasian, Commodus, Antoninus, attended with lacrymatories, lamps, bottles of liquor, and other appurtenances of affectionate superstition, which in these rural interments were wanting.

Some uncertainty there is from the period or term of burning, or the cessation of that practice. Macrobius affirmeth it was disused in his days; but most agree, though without authentic record, that it ceased with the Antonini – most safely to be understood after the reign of those emperors which assumed the name of Antoninus, extending unto Heliogabalus. Not strictly after Marcus; for about fifty years later, we find the magnificent burning and consecration of Servus; and, if we so fix this period or cessation, these urns will challenge above thirteen hundred years.

But whether this practice was only then left by emperors and great persons, or generally about Rome, and not in other provinces, we hold no authentic account; for after Tertullian, in the days of Minucius, it was obviously objected upon Christians,

---

1. *Plutarch, in Vita Lycurg.*
2. *Stowe's Survey of London*

that they condemned the practice of burning.[1] And we find a passage in Sidonius,[2] which asserteth that practice in France unto a lower account. And, perhaps, not fully disused till Christianity fully established, which gave the final extinction to these sepulchral bonfires.

Whether they were the bones of men, or women, or children, no authentic decision from ancient custom in distinct places of burial. Although not improbably conjectured, that the double sepulture, or burying-place of Abraham,[3] had in it such intention. But from exility of bones, thinness of skulls, smallness of teeth, ribs, and thigh-bones, not improbable that many thereof were persons of *minor* age, or woman. Confirmable also from things contained in them. In most were found substances resembling combs, plates like boxes, fastened with iron pins, and handsomely overwrought like the necks or bridges of musical instruments; long brass plates overwrought like the handles of neat implements; brazen nippers, to pull away hair; and in one a kind of *opale*, yet maintaining a bluish colour.

Now that they accustomed to burn or bury with them, things wherein they excelled, delighted, or which were dear unto them, either as farewells unto all pleasure, or vain apprehension that they might use them in the other world, is testified by all antiquity, observable from the gem or beryl ring upon the finger of Cynthia, the mistress of Propertius, when after her funeral pyre her ghost appeared unto him; and notably illustrated from the contents of that Roman urn preserved by Cardinal Farnese,[4] wherein besides great number of gems with heads of gods and goddesses, were found an ape of agath, a grasshopper, an elephant of amber, a crystal ball, three glasses, two spoons, and six nuts of crystal; and beyond the content of urns, in the monument of Childerek the first,[5] and fourth king from Pharamond, casually discovered three years past at Tournay, restoring unto the world much gold richly adorning his sword, two hundred rubies, many hundred imperial coins, three hundred golden bees, the bones and horse-shoes of his horse interred with him, according to the barbarous magnificence of those days in their sepulchral obsequies. Although, if we steer by the conjecture of many a Septuagint expression, some trace thereof may be found even with the ancient Hebrews, not only from the sepulchral treasure of David, but the circumcision knives which Joshua also buried.

Some men, considering the contents of these urns, lasting pieces and toys included in them, and the custom of burning with many other nations, might somewhat doubt whether all urns found among us, were properly Roman relicks, or some not belonging unto our British, Saxon, or Danish forefathers.

---

1. *"Execrantur rogos, et damnant ignium sepulturam."– Min. in Oct.*
2. *Sidon. Apollinaris.*   3. *Gen. xxiii. 4.*
4. *Vigneri Annot. in 4 Liv.*   5. *Chifflet. in Anast Childer.*

In the form of burial among the ancient Britons, the large discourses of Caesar, Tacitus, and Strabo are silent. For the discovery whereof, with other particulars, we much deplore the loss of that letter which Cicero expected or received from his brother Quintus, as a resolution of British customs; or the account which might have been made by Scribonius Largus, the physician, accompanying the Emperor Claudius, who might have also discovered that frugal bit of the old Britons,[1] which in the bigness of a bean could satisfy their thirst and hunger.

But that the Druids and ruling priests used to burn and bury, is expressed by Pomponius; that Bellinus, the brother of Brennus, and King of the Britons, was burnt, is acknowledged by Polydorus, as also by Amandus Zierexensis in *Historia* and Pineda in his *Universa Historia* (Spanish). That they held that practice in Gallia, Caesar expressly delivereth. Whether the Britons (probably descended from them, of like religion, language, and manners) did not sometimes make use of burning, or whether at least such as were after civilized unto the Roman life and manners, conformed not unto this practice, we have no historical assertion or denial. But since, from the account of Tacitus, the Romans early wrought so much civility upon the British stock, that they brought them to build temples, to wear the gown, and study the Roman laws and language, that they conformed also unto their religious rites and customs in burials, seems no improbable conjecture.

That burning the dead was used in Sarmatia is affirmed by Gaguinus; that the Sueons and Gathlanders used to burn their princes and great persons, is delivered by Saxo and Olaus; that this was the old German practice, is also asserted by Tacitus. And though we are bare in historical particulars of such obsequies in this island, or that the Saxons, Jutes, and Angles burnt their dead, yet came they from parts where 'twas of ancient practice; the Germans using it, from whom they were descended. And even in Jutland and Sleswick in Anglia Cymbrica, urns with bones were found not many years before us.

But the Danish and northern nations have raised an era or point of compute from their custom of burning their dead:[2] some deriving it from Unguinus, some from Frotho the great, who ordained by law, that princes and chief commanders should be committed unto the fire, though the common sort had the common grave interment. So Starkatterus, that old hero, was burnt, and Ringo royally burnt the body of Harold the king slain by him.

What time this custom generally expired in that nation, we discern no assured period; whether it ceased before Christianity, or upon their conversion, by Ausgurius the Gaul, in the time of Ludovicus Pius, the son of Charles the Great, according to good computes; or whether it might not be used by some persons, while for an hundred and eighty years Paganism and Christianity were

---

1. *Dionis excerpta per Xiphilin. in Severo.*
2. *Roisold, Brendetyde. Ild tyde.*

promiscuously embraced among them, there is no assured conclusion. About which times the Danes were busy in England, and particularly infested this country; where many castles and strongholds were built by them, or against them, and great number of names and families still derived from them. But since this custom was probably disused before their invasion or conquest, and the Romans confessedly practised the same since their possession of this island, the most assured account will fall upon the Romans, or Britons Romanized.

However, certain it is, that urns conceived of no Roman original, are often digged up both in Norway and Denmark, handsomely described, and graphically represented by the learned physician Wormius.[1] And in some parts of Denmark in no ordinary number, as stands delivered by authors exactly describing those countries.[2] And they contained not only bones, but many other substances in them, as knives, pieces of iron, brass, and wood, and one of Norway a brass gilded jew's-harp.

Nor were they confused or careless in disposing the noblest sort, while they placed large stones in circle about the urns or bodies which they interred: somewhat answerable unto the monument of *Rollrich* stones in England,[3] or sepulchral monument probably erected by Rollo, who after conquered Normandy; where 'tis not improbable somewhat might be discovered. Meanwhile to what nation or person belonged that large urn found at Ashbury,[4] containing mighty bones, and a buckler; what those large urns found at Little Massingham;[5] or why the Anglesea urns are placed with their mouths downward, remains yet undiscovered.

---

1. *Olai Wormii Monumenta et Antiquat. Dan.*
2. *Adolphus Cyprius in Annal. Sleswick. urnis adeo abundabat collis, etc.*
3. *In Oxfordshire, Camden.*
4. *In Cheshire, Twinus de rebus Albionicis*
5. *In Norfolk, Hollingshead.*

Chapter III

Plaistered and whited sepulchres were anciently affected in cadaverous and corrupted burials; and the rigid Jews were wont to garnish the sepulchres of the righteous.[1] Ulysses, in *Hecuba*, cared not how meanly he lived, so he might find a noble tomb after death.[2] Great princes affected great monuments; and the fair and larger urns contained no vulgar ashes, which makes that disparity in those which time discovereth among us. The present urns were not of one capacity, the largest containing above a gallon, some not much above half that measure; nor all of one figure, wherein there is no strict conformity in the same or different countries; observable from those represented by Casalius, Bosio, and others, though all found in Italy; while many have handles, ears, and long necks, but most imitate a circular figure, in a spherical and round composure; whether from any mystery, best duration or capacity, were but a conjecture. But the common form with necks was a proper figure, making our last bed like our first; nor much unlike the urns of our nativity while we lay in the nether part of the earth,[3] and inward vault of our microcosm. Many urns are red, these but of a black colour somewhat smooth, and dully sounding, which begat some doubt, whether they were burnt, or only baked in oven or sun, according to the ancient way, in many bricks, tiles, pots, and testaceous works; and, as the word *testa* is properly to be taken, when occurring without addition and chiefly intended by Pliny, when he commendeth bricks and tiles of two years old, and to make them in the spring. Nor only these concealed pieces, but the open magnificence of antiquity, ran much in the artifice of clay. Hereof the house of Mausolus was built, thus old Jupiter stood in the Capitol, and the *statua* of Hercules, made in the reign of Tarquinius Priscus, was extant in Pliny's days. And such as declined burning or funeral urns, affected coffins of clay, according to the mode of Pythagoras, a way preferred by Varro. But the spirit of great ones was above these circumscriptions, affecting copper, silver, gold, and porphyry urns, wherein Severus lay, after a serious view and sentence on that which should contain him.[4] Some of these urns were thought to have been silvered over, from sparklings in several pots, with small tinsel parcels; uncertain whether from the earth, or the first mixture in them.

Among these urns we could obtain no good account of their coverings; only one seemed arched over with some kind of brickwork. Of those found at Buxton,

---

1. *St Matt. xxiii.*

2. *Euripides.*

3. *Psal. lxiii.*

4. Χωρήσεις τὸν ἄνθρωπον, ὅν ἡ οἰκουμένη οὐκ ἐχώρησεν 'Thou shalt hold that man whom the world could not hold'. – *Dion.*

some were covered with flints, some, in other parts, with tiles; those at Yarmouth Caster were closed with Romane bricks, and some have proper earthen covers adapted and fitted to them. But in the Homerical urn of Patroclus, whatever was the solid tegument, we find the immediate covering to be a purple piece of silk: and such as had no covers might have the earth closely pressed into them, after which disposure were probably some of these, wherein we found the bones and ashes half mortared unto the sand and sides of the urn, and some long roots of quich, or dog's-grass, wreathed about the bones.

No Lamps, included liquors, lacrymatories, or tear bottles, attended these rural urns, either as sacred unto the *manes*, or passionate expressions of their surviving friends. While with rich flames, and hired tears, they solemnized their obsequies, and in the most lamented monuments made one part of their inscriptions.[1] Some find sepulchral vessels containing liquors, which time hath incrassated into jellies. For, besides these lacrymatories, notable lamps, with vessels of oils, and aromatical liquors, attended noble ossuaries; and some yet retaining a vinosity[2] and spirit in them, which, if any have tasted, they have far exceeded the palates of antiquity. Liquors not to be computed by years of annual magistrates, but by great conjunctions and the fatal periods of kingdoms.[3] The draughts of consulary date were but crude unto these, and Opimian wine[4] but in the must unto them.

In sundry graves and sepulchres we meet with rings, coins, and chalices. Ancient frugality was so severe, that they allowed no gold to attend the corpse, but only that which served to fasten their teeth.[5] Whether the Opaline stone in this were burnt upon the finger of the dead, or cast into the fire by some affectionate friend, it will consist with either custom. But other incinerable substances were found so fresh, that they could feel no singe from fire. These, upon view, were judged to be wood; but, sinking in water, and tried by the fire, we found them to be bone or ivory. In their hardness and yellow colour they most resembled box, which, in old expressions, found the epithet of eternal,[6] and perhaps in such conservatories might have passed uncorrupted.

That bay leaves were found green in the tomb of S. Humbert,[7] after an hundred and fifty years, was looked upon as miraculous. Remarkable it was unto old spectators, that the cypress of the temple of Diana lasted so many hundred years. The wood of the ark, and olive-rod of Aaron, were older at the captivity; but the cypress of the ark of Noah was the greatest vegetable of antiquity, if Josephus were not deceived by some fragments of it in his days: to omit the moor

---

1. *"Cum lacrymis posuere."*   2. *Lazius*
3. *About five hundred years.*
4. *"Vinum Opimianum annorum centum."– Petron.*
5. *12 Tabul. 1. xi. De Jure Sacro*   6. *Plin. 1. xvi.*
7. *Surius*

logs and fir trees found underground in many parts of England; the undated ruins of winds, floods, or earthquakes, and which in Flanders still show from what quarter they fell, as generally lying in a north-east position.[1]

But though we found not these pieces to be wood, according to first apprehensions, yet we missed not altogether of some woody substance; for the bones were not so clearly picked but some coals were found amongst them; a way to make wood perpetual, and a fit associate for metal, whereon was laid the foundation of the great Ephesian temple, and which were made the lasting tests of old boundaries and landmarks. Whilst we look on these, we admire not observations of coals found fresh after four hundred years.[2] In a long-deserted habitation[3] even egg-shells have been found fresh, not tending to corruption.

In the monument of King Childerick the iron relicks were found all rusty and crumbling into pieces; but our little iron pins, which fastened the ivory works, held well together, and lost not their magnetical quality, though wanting a tenacious moisture for the firmer union of parts; although it be hardly drawn into fusion, yet that metal soon submitteth unto rust and dissolution. In the brazen pieces we admired not the duration, but the freedom from rust, and ill savour, upon the hardest attrition; but now exposed unto the piercing atoms of air, in the space of a few months, they begin to spot and betray their green entrails. We conceive not these urns to have descended thus naked as they appear, or to have entered their graves without the old habit of flowers. The urn of Philopoemen was so laden with flowers and ribbons, that it afforded no sight of itself. The rigid Lycurgus allowed olive and myrtle. The Athenians might fairly except against the practice of Democritus, to be buried up in honey, as fearing to embezzle a great commodity of their country, and the best of that kind in Europe. But Plato seemed too frugally politick, who allowed no larger monument than would contain four heroick verses, and designed the most barren ground for sepulture: though we cannot commend the goodness of that sepulchral ground which was set at no higher rate than the mean salary of Judas. Though the earth had confounded the ashes of these ossuaries, yet the bones were so smartly burnt, that some thin plates of brass were found half melted among them. Whereby we apprehend they were not of the meanest caresses, perfunctorily fired, as sometimes in military, and commonly in pestilence, burnings; or after the manner of abject corpses, huddled forth and carelessly burnt, without the Esquiline Port at Rome; which was an affront continued upon Tiberius, while they but half burnt his body, and in the amphitheatre,[4] according to the custom in notable malefactors; whereas Nero seemed not so much to fear his death as that his head should be cut off and his body not burnt entire.

---

1. *Gorop. Becanus in Niloscopio.*
2. *Of Beringuccio nella pyrotechnia.*   *3. At Elham*
4. *"In amphitheatro semiustulandum."– Suetonius Vit. Tib.*

Some, finding many fragments of skulls in these urns, suspected a mixture of bones; in none we searched was there cause of such conjecture, though sometimes they declined not that practice. – The ashes of Domitian[1] were mingled with those of Julia; of Achilles with those of Patroclus. All urns contained not single ashes; without confused burnings they affectionately compounded their bones; passionately endeavouring to continue their living unions. And when distance of death denied such conjunctions, unsatisfied affections conceived some satisfaction to be neighbours in the grave, to lie urn by urn, and touch but in their manes. And many were so curious to continue their living relations, that they contrived large and family urns, wherein the ashes of their nearest friends and kindred might successively be received,[2] at least some parcels thereof, while their collateral memorials lay in minor vessels about them.

Antiquity held too light thoughts from objects of mortality, while some drew provocatives of mirth from anatomies,[3] and jugglers showed tricks with skeletons. When fiddlers made not so pleasant mirth as fencers, and men could sit with quiet stomachs, while hanging was played before them.[4] Old considerations made few *mementos* by skulls and bones upon their monuments. In the Egyptian obelisks and hieroglyphical figures it is not easy to meet with bones. The sepulchral lamps speak nothing less than sepulture, and in their literal draughts prove often obscene and antick pieces. Where we find *D. M.*[5] it is obvious to meet with sacrificing *patera's* and vessels of libation upon old sepulchral monuments. In the Jewish *hypogaeum*[6] and subterranean cell at Rome, was little observable beside the variety of lamps and frequent draughts of the Holy Candlestick. In authentic draughts of *Anthony* and *Jerome* we meet with thigh-bones and death's-heads; but the cemeterial cells of ancient Christians and martyrs were filled with draughts of Scripture stories; not declining the flourishes of cypress, palms, and olive, and the mystical figures of peacocks, doves, and cocks; but iterately affecting the portraits of Enoch, Lazarus, Jonas, and the vision of Ezekiel, as hopeful draughts, and hinting imagery of the resurrection, which is the life of the grave, and sweetens our habitations in the land of moles and pismires.

Gentle inscriptions precisely delivered the extent of men's lives, seldom the manner of their deaths, which history itself so often leaves obscure in the records of memorable persons. There is scarce any philosopher but dies twice or thrice

---

1. *Suetonius. in vita Domitian.*
2. *See the most learned and worthy Mr. M. Casubon upon Antoninus.*
3. *"Sic erimus cuncti, . . . ergo dum vivimus vivamus."*
4 *A barbarous pastime at feasts, when men stood upon a rolling globe, with their necks in a rope and a knife in their hands, ready to cut it when the stone was rolled away, wherein, if they failed, they lost their lives, to the laughter of their spectators.*
5. *Diis manibus [sacrum] (sacred to the divinised ancestor ghosts).*
6. *Bosio*

in Laertius; nor almost any life without two or three deaths in Plutarch; which makes the tragical ends of noble persons more favourably resented by compassionate readers who find some relief in the election of such differences.

The certainty of death is attended with uncertainties, in time, manner, places. The variety of monuments hath often obscured true graves; and cenotaphs confounded sepulchres. For beside their real tombs, many have found honorary and empty sepulchres. The variety of Homer's monuments made him of various countries. Euripides[1] had his tomb in Africa, but his sepulture in Macedonia. And Severus[2] found his real sepulchre in Rome, but his empty grave in Gallia.

He that lay in a golden urn[3] eminently above the earth, was not like to find the quiet of his bones. Many of these urns were broke by a vulgar discoverer in hope of enclosed treasure. The ashes of Marcellus[4] were lost above ground, upon the like account. Where profit hath prompted, no age hath wanted such miners. For which the most barbarous expilators found the most civil rhetorick. Gold once out of the earth is no more due unto it; what was unreasonably committed to the ground, is reasonably resumed from it; let monuments and rich fabricks, not riches, adorn men's ashes. The commerce of the living is not to be transferred unto the dead; it is not injustice to take that which none complains to lose, and no man is wronged where no man is possessor.

What virtue yet sleeps in this *terra damnata* and aged cinders, were petty magic to experiment. These crumbling relicks and long fired particles superannuate such expectations; bones, hairs, nails, and teeth of the dead, were the treasures of old sorcerers. In vain we revive such practices; present superstition too visibly perpetuates the folly of our forefathers, wherein unto old[5] observation this island was so complete, that it might have instructed Persia.

Plato's historian of the other world lies twelve days incorrupted, while his soul was viewing the large stations of the dead. How to keep the corpse seven days from corruption by anointing and washing, without extenteration, were an hazardable piece of art, in our choicest practice. How they made distinct separation of bones and ashes from fiery admixture, hath found no historical solution; though they seemed to make a distinct collection and overlooked not Pyrrhus his toe. Some provision they might make by fictile vessels, coverings, tiles, or flat stones, upon and about the body (and in the same field, not far from these urns, many stones were found underground), as also by careful separation of extraneous matter composing and raking up the burnt bones with forks, observable

---

1. *Pausan. in Atticis.*   2. *Lamprid. in vit. Alexand. Severi.*
3. *Trajanus. – Dion.*
4. *Plut. in vit. Marcelli. The commission of the Gothish King Theodoric for finding out sepulchral treasure. – Cassiodor. var. I. 4.*
5. *Britannia hodie eam attonite celebrat tantis ceremoniis ut dedisse Persis videri possit.– Plin. I. 29.*

40

in that notable lamp of Galvanus[1]. Martianus, who had the sight of the *vas ustrinum*[2] or vessel wherein they burnt the dead, found in the Esquiline field at Rome, might have afforded clearer solution. But their insatisfaction herein begat that remarkable invention in the funeral pyres of some princes, by incombustible sheets made with a texture of asbestos, incremable flax, or salamander's wool, which preserved their bones and ashes incommixed.

How the bulk of a man should sink into so few pounds of bones and ashes, may seem strange unto any who considers not its constitution, and how slender a mass will remain upon an open and urging fire of the carnal composition. Even bones themselves, reduced into ashes, do abate a notable proportion. And consisting much of a volatile salt, when that is fired out, make a light kind of cinders. Although their bulk be disproportionable to their weight, when the heavy principle of salt is fired out, and the earth almost only remaineth; observable in sallow, which makes more ashes than oak, and discovers the common fraud of selling ashes by measure, and not by ponderation.

Some bones make best skeletons,[3] some bodies quick and speediest ashes. Who would expect a quick flame from hydropical Heraclitus? The poisoned soldier when his belly brake, put out two pyres in Plutarch.[4] But in the plague of Athens,[5] one private pyre served two or three intruders; and the Saracens burnt in large heaps, by the king of Castile,[6] showed how little fuel sufficeth. Though the funeral pyre of Patroclus took up an hundred foot,[7] a piece of an old boat burnt Pompey; and if the burthen of Isaac were sufficient for an holocaust, a man may carry his own pyre.

From animals are drawn good burning lights, and good medicines against burning.[8] Though the seminal humour seems of a contrary nature to fire, yet the body completed proves a combustible lump, wherein fire finds flame even from bones, and some fuel almost from all parts; though the metropolis of humidity[9] seems least disposed unto it, which might render the skulls of these urns less burned than other bones. But all flies or sinks before fire almost in all bodies: when the common ligament is dissolved, the attenuable parts ascend, the rest subside in coal, calx, or ashes.

To burn the bones of the king of Edom for lime,[10] seems no irrational ferity; but to drink of the ashes of dead relations,[11] a passionate prodigality. He that hath the ashes of his friend, hath an everlasting treasure; where fire taketh leave,

---

1. *To be seen in Licet. de reconditis veterum lucernis (p.599, fol.1653)*
2. *Typograph. Roma et Martiano.*
3. *Old bones according to Lyserus. Those of young persons not tall nor fat according to Columbus.*
4. *In vita Gracc.*   5. *Thucydides*   6. *Laurent. Valla.*
7. Ἑκατόμπεδον ἔνϑα ῆ ἔνϑα *(Iliad 23.)*   8. *Sperm ran. Alb. Ovor.*
9. *The Brain. Hippocrates.*   10. *Amos ii. 1.*
11. *As Artemisia of her husband Mausolus.*

corruption slowly enters. In bones well burnt, fire makes a wall against itself; experimented in Cupels,[1] and tests of metals, which consist of such ingredients. What the sun compoundeth, fire analyzeth, not transmuteth. That devouring agent leaves almost always a morsel for the earth, whereof all things are but a colony; and which, if time permits, the mother element will have in their primitive mass again.

He that looks for urns and old sepulchral relicks, must not seek them in the ruins of temples, where no religion anciently placed them. These were found in a field, according to ancient custom, in noble or private burial; the old practice of the Canaanites, the family of Abraham, and the burying-place of Joshua, in the borders of his possessions; and also agreeable unto Roman practice to bury by highways, whereby their monuments were under eye: memorials of themselves, and *memento's* of mortality unto living passengers; whom the epitaphs of great ones were fain to beg to stay and look upon them – a language though sometimes used, not so proper in church inscriptions.[2] The sensible rhetorick of the dead, to exemplarity of good life, first admitted to the bones of pious men and martyrs within church walls, which in succeeding ages crept into promiscuous practice: while Constantine was peculiarly favoured to be admitted into the church porch, and the first thus buried in England, was in the days of Cuthred.

Christians dispute how their bodies should lie in the grave.[23] In urnal interment they clearly escaped this controversy. Though we decline the religious consideration, yet in cemeterial and narrower burying-places, to avoid confusion and cross-position, a certain posture were to be admitted: which even Pagan civility observed. The Persians lay north and south; the Megarians and Phoenicians placed their heads to the east; the Athenians, some think, towards the west, which Christians still retain. And Beda will have it to be the posture of our Saviour. That he was crucified with his face toward the west, we will not contend with tradition and probable account; but we applaud not the hand of the painter, in exalting his cross so high above those on either side: since hereof we find no authentic account in history, and even the crosses found by Helena, pretend no such distinction from longitude or dimension.

To be knav'd out of our graves, to have our skulls made drinking-bowls, and our bones turned into pipes, to delight and sport our enemies, are tragical abominations escaped in burning burials.

Urnal interments and burnt relicks lie not in fear of worms, or to be an heritage for serpents. In carnal sepulture, corruptions seem peculiar unto parts; and some speak of snakes out of the spinal marrow. But while we suppose common worms in graves, 'tis not easy to find any there; few in churchyards above a foot deep, fewer or none in churches though in fresh-decayed bodies. Teeth, bones,

---

1. *A chemical vessel made of earth, ashes, or burnt bones, and in which assay-masters try their metals.*

2. *Siste viator.* 3. *Kirkmasnnus de funer*

and hair, give the most lasting defiance to corruption. In an hydropical body, ten years buried in the churchyard, we met with a fat concretion, where the nitre of the earth, and the salt and lixivious liquor of the body, had coagulated large lumps of fat into the consistence of the hardest Castile soap, whereof part remaineth with us.[1] After a battle with the Persians, the Roman corpses decayed in few days, while the Persian bodies remained dry and uncorrupted. Bodies in the same ground do not uniformly dissolve, nor bones equally moulder; whereof in the opprobrious disease, we expect no long duration. The body of the Marquis of Dorset[2] seemed sound and handsomely cere-clothed, that after seventy-eight years was found uncorrupted. Common tombs preserve not beyond powder: a firmer consistence and compage of parts might be expected from arefaction, deep burial, or charcoal. The greatest antiquities of mortal bodies may remain in putrefied bones, whereof, though we take not in the pillar of Lot's wife, or metamorphosis of Ortelius[3], some may be older than pyramids, in the putrefied relicks of the general inundation. When Alexander opened the tomb of Cyrus, the remaining bones discovered his proportion, whereof urnal fragments afford but a bad conjecture, and have this disadvantage of grave interments, that they leave us ignorant of most personal discoveries. For since bones afford not only rectitude and stability but figure unto the body, it is no impossible physiognomy to conjecture at fleshy appendencies, and after what shape the muscles and carnous parts might hang in their full consistencies. A full-spread *cariola*[4] shows a well-shaped horse behind; handsome formed skulls give some analogy of fleshy resemblance. A critical view of bones makes a good distinction of sexes. Even colour is not beyond conjecture, since it is hard to be deceived in the distinction of the Negroes' skulls.[5] Dante's[6] characters are to be found in skulls as well as faces. Hercules is not only known by his foot. Other parts make out their comproportions and inferences upon whole or parts. And since the dimensions of the head measure the whole body, and the figure thereof gives conjecture of the principal faculties: physiognomy outlives ourselves, and ends not in our graves.

Severe contemplators, observing these lasting relicks, may think them good

---

1. *Known to French chemists by the name "adipocire," this substance was first discovered by Sir Thomas Browne.*
2. *Thomas, Marquis of Dorset, was buried in 1530, then dug up in 1608, and found perfect and nothing corrupted, the flesh not hardened, but in colour, proportion and softness like an ordinary corpse newly interred. (see Burton's Description of Leicestershire)*
3. *In his map of Russia.*
4. *That part in the skeleton of a horse, which is made by the haunch-bones.*
5. *For their extraordinary thickness. The remark in the text is more corrrect than the note's explanation of it. Such measurements as facial angle are a more accurate means of differentiation.*
6. *Purgat. xxiii. 31.*

monuments of persons past, little advantage to future beings; and, considering that power which subdueth all things unto itself, that can resume the scattered atoms, or identify out of anything, conceive it superfluous to expect a resurrection out of relicks: but the soul subsisting, other matter, clothed with due accidents, may salve the individuality. Yet the saints, we observe, arose from graves and monuments about the holy city. Some think the ancient patriarchs so earnestly desired to lay their bones in Canaan, as hoping to make a part of that resurrection; and, though thirty miles from Mount Calvary, at least to lie in that region which should produce the first-fruits of the dead. And if, according to learned conjecture, the bodies of men shall rise where their greatest relicks remain, many are not like to err in the topography of their resurrection, though their bones or bodies be after translated by angels into the field of Ezekiel's vision, or as some will order it, into the valley of judgment, or Jehosaphat.[1]

---

1. *Tirin. in Ezek.*

Chapter IV

Christians have handsomely glossed the deformity of death by careful consideration of the body, and civil rites which take off brutal terminations: and though they conceived all reparable by a resurrection, cast not off all care of interment. And since the ashes of sacrifices burnt upon the altar of God, were carefully carried out by the priests, and deposed in a clean field; since they acknowledged their bodies to be the lodging of Christ, and temples of the Holy Ghost, they devolved not all upon the sufficiency of soul-existence; and therefore with long services and full solemnities, concluded their last exequies, wherein to all distinctions the Greek devotion seems most pathetically ceremonious.[1]

Christian invention hath chiefly driven at rites, which speak hopes of another life, and hints of a resurrection. And if the ancient Gentiles held not the immortality of their better part, and some subsistence after death, in several rites, customs, actions, and expressions, they contradicted their own opinions: wherein Democritus went high, even to the thought of a resurrection, as scoffingly recorded by Pliny.[2] What can be more express than the expression of Phocylides?[3] Or who would expect from Lucretius[4] a sentence of Ecclesiastes? Before Plato could speak, the soul had wings in Homer, which fell not, but flew out of the body into the mansions of the dead; who also observed that handsome distinction of Demas and Soma, for the body conjoined to the soul, and body separated from it. Lucian spoke much truth in jest, when he said that part of Hercules which proceeded from Alcmena perished, that from Jupiter remained immortal. Thus Socrates[5] was content that his friends should bury his body, so they would not think they buried Socrates; and, regarding only his immortal part, was indifferent to be burnt or buried. From such considerations, Diogenes might contemn sepulture, and, being satisfied that the soul could not perish, grow careless of corporal interment. The Stoics, who thought the souls of wise men had their habitation about the moon, might make slight account of subterraneous deposition; whereas the Pythagoreans and transcorporating philosophers, who were to be often buried, held great care of their interment. And the Platonicks rejected not a due care of the grave, though they put their ashes to unreasonable expectations, in their tedious term of return and long set revolution.

---

1. *Rituale Graecum, opera J Goar, in officio exequiarum*

2. *"Similis . . . reviviscendi promissa Democrito vanitas, qui non revixit ipse. Quae (malum) ista dementia est iterari vitam morte?"– Plin. I. vii. c. 55.*

3. *Καὶ τάχα δ'ἐκ γαίης ἐλπίζομεν ἐς φάος ἐλθεῖν λείψαν ἀποιχομένων, et deinceps. Pseudo-Phocylides, Sententiae*

4. *"Cedit item retro de terra quod fuit ante in terras."– Luc., lib. ii. 998.*

5. *Plato in Phaedo*

Men have lost their reason in nothing so much as their religion, wherein stones and clouts make martyrs; and, since the religion of one seems madness unto another, to afford an account or rational of old rites requires no rigid reader. That they kindled the pyre aversely, or turning their face from it, was an handsome symbol of unwilling ministration. That they washed their bones with wine and milk; that the mother wrapped them in linen, and dried them in her bosom, the first fostering part and place of their nourishment; that they opened their eyes toward heaven before they kindled the fire, as the place of their hopes or original, were no improper ceremonies. Their last valediction,[1] thrice uttered by the attendants, was also very solemn, and somewhat answered by Christians, who thought it too little, if they threw not the earth thrice upon the interred body. That, in strewing their tombs, the Romans affected the rose; the Greeks *amaranthus* and myrtle: that the funeral pyre consisted of sweet fuel, cypress, fir, larix, yew, and trees perpetually verdant, lay silent expressions of their surviving hopes. Wherein Christians, who deck their coffins with bays, have found a more elegant emblem; for that it, seeming dead, will restore itself from the root, and its dry and exsuccous leaves resume their verdure again; which, if we mistake not, we have also observed in furze. Whether the planting of yew in churchyards hold not its original from ancient funeral rites, or as an emblem of resurrection, from its perpetual verdure, may also admit conjecture.

They made use of musick to excite or quiet the affections of their friends, according to different harmonies. But the secret and symbolical hint was the harmonical nature of the soul; which, delivered from the body, went again to enjoy the primitive harmony of heaven, from whence it first descended; which, according to its progress traced by antiquity, came down by Cancer, and ascended by Capricornus.

They burnt not children before their teeth appeared, as apprehending their bodies too tender a morsel for fire, and that their gristly bones would scarce leave separable relicks after the pyral combustion. That they kindled not fire in their houses for some days after was a strict memorial of the late afflicting fire. And mourning without hope, they had an happy fraud against excessive lamentation, by a common opinion that deep sorrows disturb their ghosts.[2]

That they buried their dead on their backs, or in a supine position, seems agreeable unto profound sleep, and common posture of dying; contrary to the most natural way of birth; nor unlike our pendulous posture, in the doubtful state of the womb. Diogenes was singular, who preferred a prone situation in the grave; and some Christians[3] like neither, who decline the figure of rest, and make choice of an erect posture.

---

1. *"Vale, vale, nos te ordine quo natura permittet sequamur."*
2. *"Tu manes ne loede meos."*
3. *The Russians. etc*

That they carried them out of the world with their feet forward, not inconsonant unto reason, as contrary unto the native posture of man, and his production first into it; and also agreeable unto their opinions, while they bid adieu unto the world, not to look again upon it; whereas Mahometans who think to return to a delightful life again, are carried forth with their heads forward, and looking toward their houses.

They closed their eyes, as parts which first die, or first discover the sad effects of death. But their iterated clamations to excitate their dying or dead friends, or revoke them unto life again, was a vanity of affection; as not presumably ignorant of the critical tests of death, by apposition of feathers, glasses, and reflection of figures, which dead eyes represent not: which, however not strictly verifiable in fresh and warm *cadavers*, could hardly elude the test, in corpses of four or five days.[1]

That they sucked in the last breath of their expiring friends, was surely a practice of no medical institution, but a loose opinion that the soul passed out that way, and a fondness of affection, from some Pythagorical foundation,[2] that the spirit of one body passed into another, which they wished might be their own.

That they poured oil upon the pyre, was a tolerable practice, while the intention rested in facilitating the ascension. But to place good omens in the quick and speedy burning, to sacrifice unto the winds for a despatch in this office, was a low form of superstition.

The *Archimime*, or jester, attending the funeral train, and imitating the speeches, gesture, and manners of the deceased, was too light for such solemnities, contradicting their funeral orations and doleful rites of the grave.

That they buried a piece of money with them as a fee of the Elysian ferryman, was a practice full of folly. But the ancient custom of placing coins in considerable urns, and the present practice of burying medals in the noble foundations of Europe, are laudable ways of historical discoveries, in actions, persons, chronologies; and posterity will applaud them.

We examine not the old laws of sepulture, exempting certain persons from burial or burning. But hereby we apprehend that these were not the bones of persons planet-struck or burnt with fire from heaven; no relicks of traitors to their country, self-killers, or sacrilegious malefactors; persons in old apprehension unworthy of the earth; condemned unto the Tartarus of hell, and bottomless pit of Pluto, from whence there was no redemption.

Nor were only many customs questionable in order to their obsequies, but also sundry practices, fictions, and conceptions, discordant or obscure, of their state and future beings. Whether unto eight or ten bodies of men to add one of a woman, as being more inflammable and unctuously constituted for the

---

1. *At least by some difference from living eyes.*
2. *Francresco Perucci, Pompe funebri.*

better pyral combustion, were any rational practice; or whether the complaint of Periander's wife be tolerable, that wanting her funeral burning, she suffered intolerable cold in hell, according to the constitution of the infernal house of Pluto, wherein cold makes a great part of their tortures; it cannot pass without some question.

Why the female ghosts appear unto Ulysses, before the heroes and masculine spirits – why the Psyche or soul of Tiresias is of the masculine gender,[1] who, being blind on earth, sees more than all the rest in hell; why the funeral suppers consisted of eggs, beans, smallage, and lettuce, since the dead are made to eat asphodels[2] about the Elysian meadows:– why, since there is no sacrifice acceptable, nor any propitiation for the covenant of the grave, men set up the deity of *Morta*, and fruitlessly adored divinities without ears, it cannot escape some doubt.

The dead seem all alive in the human Hades of Homer, yet cannot well speak, prophecy, or know the living, except they drink blood, wherein is the life of man. And therefore the souls of Penelope's paramours, conducted by Mercury, chirped like bats, and those which followed Hercules, made a noise but like a flock of birds.

The departed spirits know things past and to come; yet are ignorant of things present. Agamemnon foretells what should happen unto Ulysses; yet ignorantly inquires what is become of his own son. The ghosts are afraid of swords in Homer; yet Sibylla tells Æneas in Virgil, the thin habit of spirits was beyond the force of weapons. The spirits put off their malice with their bodies, and Caesar and Pompey accord in Latin hell; yet Ajax, in Homer, endures not a conference with Ulysses; and Deiphobus appears all mangled in Virgil's ghosts, yet we meet with perfect shadows among the wounded ghosts of Homer.

Since Charon in Lucian applauds his condition among the dead, whether it be handsomely said of Achilles, that living contemner of death, that he had rather be a ploughman's servant, than emperor of the dead? How Hercules his soul is in hell, and yet in heaven; and Julius his soul in a star, yet seen by Æneas in hell? – except the ghosts were but images and shadows of the soul, received in higher mansions, according to the ancient division of body, soul, and image, or *simulachrum* of them both. The particulars of future beings must needs be dark unto ancient theories, which Christian philosophy yet determines but in a cloud of opinions. A dialogue between two infants in the womb concerning the state of this world, might handsomely illustrate our ignorance of the next, whereof methinks we yet discourse in Pluto's den, and are but embryo philosophers.

Pythagoras escapes in the fabulous hell of Dante,[3] among that swarm of philosophers, wherein, whilst we meet with Plato and Socrates, Cato is to be

---

1. In Homer.   *2. In Lucian.*   *3. Del Inferno, cant. 4.*

found in no lower place than purgatory. Among all the set, Epicurus is most considerable, whom men make honest without an Elysium, who contemned life without encouragement of immortality, and making nothing after death, yet made nothing of the king of terrors.

Were the happiness of the next world as closely apprehended as the felicities of this, it were a martyrdom to live; and unto such as consider none hereafter, it must be more than death to die, which makes us amazed at those audacities that durst be nothing and return into their *chaos* again. Certainly such spirits as could contemn death, when they expected no better being after, would have scorned to live, had they known any. And therefore we applaud not the judgment of Machiavel, that Christianity makes men cowards, or that with the confidence of but half-dying, the despised virtues of patience and humility have abased the spirits of men, which Pagan principles exalted; but rather regulated the wildness of audacities in the attempts, grounds, and eternal sequels of death; wherein men of the boldest spirits are often prodigiously temerarious. Nor can we extenuate the valour of ancient martyrs, who contemned death in the uncomfortable scene of their lives, and in their decrepit martyrdoms did probably lose not many months of their days, or parted with life when it was scarce worth the living. For (beside that long time past holds no consideration unto a slender time to come) they had no small disadvantage from the constitution of old age, which naturally makes men fearful, and complexionally superannuated from the bold and courageous thoughts of youth and fervent years. But the contempt of death from corporal animosity, promoteth not our felicity. They may sit in the orchestra, and noblest seats of heaven, who have held up shaking hands in the fire, and humanly contended for glory.

Meanwhile Epicurus lies deep in Dante's hell, wherein we meet with tombs enclosing souls which denied their immortalities. But whether the virtuous heathen, who lived better than he spake, or erring in the principles of himself, yet lived above philosophers of more specious maxims, lie so deep as he is placed; at least so low as not to rise against Christians, who believing or knowing that truth, have lastingly denied it in their practice and conversation – were a query too sad to insist on.

But all or most apprehensions rested in opinions of some future being, which, ignorantly or coldly believed, begat those perverted conceptions, ceremonies, sayings, which Christians pity or laugh at. Happy are they which live not in that disadvantage of time, when men could say little for futurity, but from reason: whereby the noblest minds fell often upon doubtful deaths, and melancholy dissolutions. With these hopes, Socrates warmed his doubtful spirits against that cold potion; and Cato, before he durst give the fatal stroke, spent part of the night in reading the Immortality of Plato, thereby confirming his wavering hand unto the animosity of that attempt.

It is the heaviest stone that melancholy can throw at a man, to tell him he is at the end of his nature; or that there is no further state to come, unto which this seems progressional, and otherwise made in vain. Without this accomplishment, the natural expectation and desire of such a state, were but a fallacy in nature; unsatisfied considerators would quarrel the justice of their constitutions, and rest content that Adam had fallen lower; whereby, by knowing no other original, and deeper ignorance of themselves, they might have enjoyed the happiness of inferior creatures, who in tranquillity possess their constitutions, as having not the apprehension to deplore their own natures, and, being framed below the circumference of these hopes, or cognition of better being, the wisdom of God hath necessitated their contentment: but the superior ingredient and obscured part of ourselves, whereto all present felicities afford no resting contentment, will be able at last to tell us, we are more than our present selves, and evacuate such hopes in the fruition of their own accomplishments.

Chapter V

Now since these dead bones have already outlasted the living ones of Methuselah, and in a yard underground, and thin walls of clay, outworn all the strong and specious buildings above it; and quietly rested under the drums and tramplings of three conquests: what prince can promise such diuturnity unto his relicks, or might not gladly say,

Sic ego componi versus in ossa velim?[1]

Time, which antiquates antiquities, and hath an art to make dust of all things, hath yet spared these minor monuments.

In vain we hope to be known by open and visible conservatories, when to be unknown was the means of their continuation, and obscurity their protection. If they died by violent hands, and were thrust into their urns, these bones become considerable, and some old philosophers would honour them,[2] whose souls they conceived most pure, which were thus snatched from their bodies, and to retain a stronger propension unto them; whereas they weariedly left a languishing corpse and with faint desires of reunion. If they fell by long and aged decay, yet wrapt up in the bundle of time, they fall into indistinction, and make but one blot with infants. If we begin to die when we live, and long life be but a prolongation of death, our life is a sad composition; we live with death, and die not in a moment. How many pulses made up the life of Methuselah, were work for Archimedes: common counters sum up the life of Moses his man.[3] Our days become considerable, like petty sums, by minute accumulations: where numerous fractions make up but small round numbers; and our days of a span long, make not one little finger.[4]

If the nearness of our last necessity brought a nearer conformity into it, there were a happiness in hoary hairs, and no calamity in half-senses. But the long habit of living indisposeth us for dying; when avarice makes us the sport of death, when even David grew politickly cruel, and Solomon could hardly be said to be the wisest of men. But many are too early old, and before the date of age. Adversity stretcheth our days, misery makes Alcmena's nights,[5] and time hath no wings unto it. But the most tedious being is that which can unwish itself, content to be nothing, or never to have been, which was beyond the malcontent of Job, who cursed not the day of his life, but his nativity; content to have so far been, as

---

1. *Tibullus, lib. iii. el. 2, 26.*

2. *Oracula Chaldaica cum scholis Pselli et Phethonis.*

3. *In the Psalm of Moses (Psalm 90).*

4. *According to the ancient arithmetick of the hand, wherein the little finger of the right hand contracted, signified an hundred. – Pierius in Hieroglyph.*

5. *One night as long as three.*

to have a title to future being, although he had lived here but in an hidden state of life, and as it were an abortion.

What song the Syrens sang, or what name Achilles assumed when he hid himself among women, though puzzling questions,[1] are not beyond all conjecture. What time the persons of these ossuaries entered the famous nations of the dead,[2] and slept with princes and counsellors, might admit a wide solution. But who were the proprietaries of these bones, or what bodies these ashes made up, were a question above antiquarism; not to be resolved by man, nor easily perhaps by spirits, except we consult the provincial guardians, or tutelary observators. Had they made as good provision for their names, as they have done for their relicks, they had not so grossly erred in the art of perpetuation. But to subsist in bones, and be but pyramidally extant, is a fallacy in duration. Vain ashes which in the oblivion of names, persons, times, and sexes, have found unto themselves a fruitless continuation, and only arise unto late posterity, as emblems of mortal vanities, antidotes against pride, vain-glory, and madding vices. Pagan vain-glories which thought the world might last for ever, had encouragement for ambition; and, finding no *atropos* unto the immortality of their names, were never dampt with the necessity of oblivion. Even old ambitions had the advantage of ours, in the attempts of their vain-glories, who acting early, and before the probable meridian of time, have by this time found great accomplishment of their designs, whereby the ancient heroes have already outlasted their monuments and mechanical preservations. But in this latter scene of time, we cannot expect such mummies unto our memories, when ambition may fear the prophecy of Elias,[3] and Charles the Fifth can never hope to live within two Methuselahs of Hector.[4]

And therefore, restless inquietude for the diuturnity of our memories unto the present considerations seems a vanity almost out of date, and superannuated piece of folly. We cannot hope to live so long in our names, as some have done in their persons. One face of Janus holds no proportion unto the other. 'Tis too late to be ambitious. The great mutations of the world are acted, or time may be too short for our designs. To extend our memories by monuments, whose death we daily pray for, and whose duration we cannot hope, without injury to our expectations in the advent of the last day, were a contradiction to our beliefs. We whose generations are ordained in this setting part of time, are providentially taken off from such imaginations; and, being necessitated to eye the remaining particle of futurity, are naturally constituted unto thoughts of the next world, and cannot excusably decline the consideration of that duration, which maketh pyramids pillars of snow, and all that's past a moment.

---

1. *The puzzling questions of Tiberius unto grammarians. – Marcel. Donatus in Suet.*
2. Κλυτὰ ἔθνεα νεκρῶν. *Hom.*
3. *That the world may last but six thousand years.*
4. *Hector's fame outlasting above two lives of Methuselah before that famous prince was extant.*

Circles and right lines limit and close all bodies, and the mortal right-lined circle[1] must conclude and shut up all. There is no antidote against the opium of time, which temporally considereth all things: our fathers find their graves in our short memories, and sadly tell us how we may be buried in our survivors. Gravestones tell truth scarce forty years.[2] Generations pass while some trees stand, and old families last not three oaks. To be read by bare inscriptions like many in Gruter,[3] to hope for eternity by enigmatical epithets or first letters of our names, to be studied by antiquaries, who we were, and have new names given us like many of the mummies, are cold consolations unto the students of perpetuity, even by everlasting languages.

To be content that times to come should only know there was such a man, not caring whether they knew more of him, was a frigid ambition in Cardan;[4] disparaging his horoscopal inclination and judgment of himself. Who cares to subsist like Hippocrates's patients, or Achilles's horses in Homer, under naked nominations, without deserts and noble acts, which are the balsam of our memories, the *entelechia* and soul of our subsistences? To be nameless in worthy deeds, exceeds an infamous history. The Canaanitish woman lives more happily without a name, than Herodias with one. And who had not rather have been the good thief, than Pilate?

But the iniquity of oblivion blindly scattereth her poppy, and deals with the memory of men without distinction to merit of perpetuity. Who can but pity the founder of the pyramids? Herostratus lives that burnt the temple of Diana, he is almost lost that built it. Time hath spared the epitaph of Adrian's horse, confounded that of himself. In vain we compute our felicities by the advantage of our good names, since bad have equal durations, and Thersites is like to live as long as Agamemnon without the favour of the everlasting register. Who knows whether the best of men be known, or whether there be not more remarkable persons forgot, than any that stand remembered in the known account of time? The first man had been as unknown as the last, and Methuselah's long life had been his only chronicle.

Oblivion is not to be hired. The greater part must be content to be as though they had not been, to be found in the register of God, not in the record of man. Twenty-seven names make up the first story and the recorded names ever since contain not one living century. The number of the dead long exceedeth all that shall live. The night of time far surpasseth the day, and who knows when was the equinox? Every hour adds unto that current arithmetick, which scarce stands one moment. And since death must be the *Lucina* of life, and even Pagans[5] could

---

1. *The character of death.*
2. *Old ones being taken up, and other bodies laid under them.*
3. *Grutori Inscriptiones Antiquae.*
4. *"Cuperem notum esse quod sim non opto ut sciatur qualis sim."*
5. *Euripides.*

doubt, whether thus to live were to die; since our longest sun sets at right descensions, and makes but winter arches, and therefore it cannot be long before we lie down in darkness, and have our light in ashes;[1] since the brother of death[2] daily haunts us with dying *mementoes*, and time that grows old in itself, bids us hope no long duration; – diuturnity[3] is a dream and folly of expectation.

Darkness and light divide the course of time, and oblivion shares with memory a great part even of our living beings; we slightly remember our felicities, and the smartest strokes of affliction leave but short smart upon us. Sense endureth no extremities, and sorrows destroy us or themselves. To weep into stones are fables. Afflictions induce callosities; miseries are slippery, or fall like snow upon us, which notwithstanding is no unhappy stupidity. To be ignorant of evils to come, and forgetful of evils past, is a merciful provision in nature, whereby we digest the mixture of our few and evil days, and, our delivered senses not relapsing into cutting remembrances, our sorrows are not kept raw by the edge of repetitions. A great part of antiquity contented their hopes of subsistency with a transmigration of their souls – a good way to continue their memories, while having the advantage of plural successions, they could not but act something remarkable in such variety of beings, and enjoying the fame of their passed selves, make accumulation of glory unto their last durations. Others, rather than be lost in the uncomfortable night of nothing, were content to recede into the common being, and make one particle of the public soul of all things, which was no more than to return into their unknown and divine original again. Egyptian ingenuity was more unsatisfied, contriving their bodies in sweet consistences, to attend the return of their souls. But all is vanity, feeding the wind, and folly. Egyptian mummies, which Cambyses or time hath spared, avarice now consumeth. Mummy is become merchandise, *Mizraim* cures wounds, and *Pharaoh* is sold for balsams.

In vain do individuals hope for immortality, or any patent from oblivion, in preservations below the moon: Men have been deceived even in their flatteries, above the sun, and studied conceits to perpetuate their names in heaven. The various cosmography of that part hath already varied the names of contrived constellations; Nimrod is lost in Orion, and Osyris in the Dog-star. While we look for incorruption in the heavens, we find that they are but like the earth; – durable in their main bodies, alterable in their parts; whereof, beside comets and new stars, perspectives begin to tell tales, and the spots that wander about the sun, with Phaeton's favour, would make clear conviction.

There is nothing strictly immortal, but immortality. Whatever hath no beginning, may be confident of no end; – all others have a dependent being and within the reach of destruction; – which is the peculiar of that necessary essence that cannot destroy itself; – and the highest strain of omnipotency, to be

---

1. *According to the custom of the Jews, who placed a lighted wax-candle in a pot of ashes by the corpse.*
2. *That is, Sleep.*   3. *the quality or state of being continuous or lasting.*

so powerfully constituted as not to suffer even from the power of itself. But the sufficiency of Christian immortality frustrates all earthly glory, and the quality of either state after death, makes a folly of posthumous memory. God who can only destroy our souls, and hath assured our resurrection, either of our bodies or names hath directly promised no duration. Wherein there is so much of chance, that the boldest expectants have found unhappy frustration; and to hold long subsistence, seems but a scape in oblivion. But man is a noble animal, splendid in ashes, and pompous in the grave, solemnizing nativities and deaths with equal lustre, nor omitting ceremonies of bravery in the infamy of his nature.

Life is a pure flame, and we live by an invisible sun within us. A small fire sufficeth for life, great flames seemed too little after death, while men vainly affected precious pyres, and to burn like Sardanapalus; but the wisdom of funeral laws found the folly of prodigal blazes and reduced undoing fires unto the rule of sober obsequies, wherein few could be so mean as not to provide wood, pitch, a mourner, and an urn.

Five languages secured not the epitaph of Gordianus.[1] The man of God lives longer without a tomb than any by one, invisibly interred by angels, and adjudged to obscurity, though not without some marks directing human discovery. Enoch and Elias, without either tomb or burial, in an anomalous state of being, are the great examples of perpetuity, in their long and living memory, in strict account being still on this side death, and having a late part yet to act upon this stage of earth. If in the decretory term of the world we shall not all die but be changed, according to received translation, the last day will make but few graves; at least quick resurrections will anticipate lasting sepultures. Some graves will be opened before they be quite closed, and Lazarus be no wonder. When many that feared to die, shall groan that they can die but once, the dismal state is the second and living death, when life puts despair on the damned; when men shall wish the coverings of mountains, not of monuments, and annihilations shall be courted.

While some have studied monuments, others have studiously declined them, and some have been so vainly boisterous, that they durst not acknowledge their graves; wherein Alaricus[2] seems most subtle, who had a river turned to hide his bones at the bottom. Even Sylla, that thought himself safe in his urn, could not prevent revenging tongues, and stones thrown at his monument. Happy are they whom privacy makes innocent, who deal so with men in this world, that they are not afraid to meet them in the next; who, when they die, make no commotion among the dead, and are not touched with that poetical taunt of Isaiah.[3]

Pyramids, arches, obelisks, were but the irregularities of vain-glory, and wild enormities of ancient magnanimity. But the most magnanimous resolution rests

---

1. *Greek, Latin, Hebrew, Egyptian, Arabic defaced by the Emperor Licinius.*
2. *Jornandes de rebus Geticis*
3. *Isa. xiv. 16: 'Is this the man that made the earth to tremble, that did shake kingdoms...'*

in the Christian religion, which trampleth upon pride and sits on the neck of ambition, humbly pursuing that infallible perpetuity, unto which all others must diminish their diameters, and be poorly seen in angles of contingency.[1]

Pious spirits who passed their days in raptures of futurity, made little more of this world, than the world that was before it, while they lay obscure in the chaos of preordination, and night of their forebeings. And if any have been so happy as truly to understand Christian annihilation, ecstasies, exolution, liquefaction, transformation, the kiss of the spouse, gustation of God, and ingression into the divine shadow, they have already had an handsome anticipation of heaven; the glory of the world is surely over, and the earth in ashes unto them.

To subsist in lasting monuments, to live in their productions, to exist in their names and predicament of chimeras, was large satisfaction unto old expectations, and made one part of their Elysiums. But all this is nothing in the metaphysicks of true belief. To live indeed, is to be again ourselves, which being not only an hope, but an evidence in noble believers, 'tis all one to lie in St Innocent's[2] church-yard as in the sands of Egypt. Ready to be anything, in the ecstasy of being ever, and as content with six foot as the moles of Adrianus.[3]

Tabesne cadavera solvat,
An rogus, haud refert.
Lucan. viii. 809.

FINIS

---

1. *Angelus contingentiae – the least of angles.*
2. *In Paris, where bodies soon consume.*
3. *A stately mausoleum or sepulchral pile, built by Adrianus in Rome, where now standeth the castle of St Angelo.*

The Garden of Cyrus

OR,

The Quincunciall, Lozenge,
or Net-work Plantations of the Ancients,
Artificially, Naturally, Mystically Considered

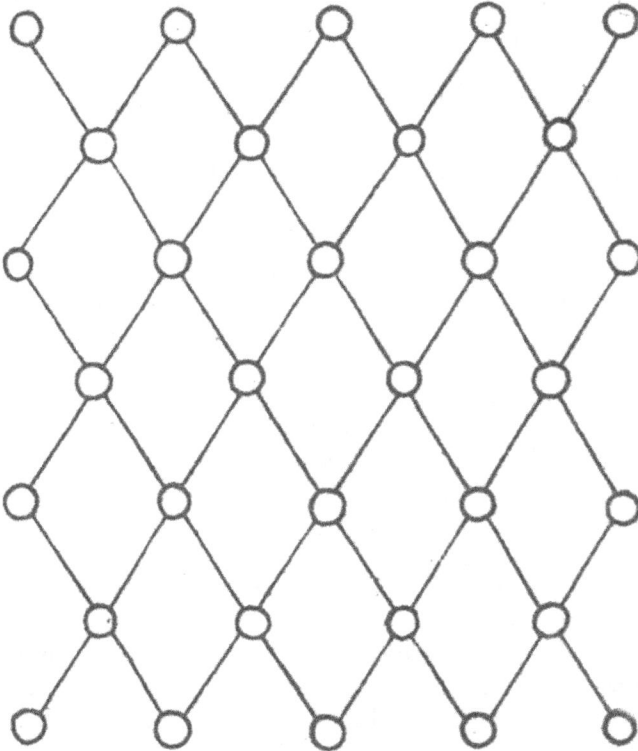

Quid Quincunce speciosus, qui, in quamcunque partem spectaveris, rectus est?
– Quintillian. Institutio Oratoria VIII.3.ix:

*(What more beautiful than the quincunx [planting], that,
however it is viewed, presents straight lines?)*

To My
Worthy and Honoured Friend
NICHOLAS BACON
Of Gillingham Esquire.

Had I not observed that Purblinde[1] men have discoursed well of sight, and some[2] without issue, excellently of Generation; I that was never master of any considerable garden, had not attempted this Subject. But the Earth is the Garden of Nature, and each fruitfull Countrey a Paradise. Dioscorides made most of his Observations in his march about with Antonius; and Theophrastus raised his generalities chiefly from the field.

Beside we write no Herball, nor can this Volume deceive you, who have handled the massiest[3] thereof: who know that three Folio's[4] are yet too little, and how new Herbals fly from America upon us, from persevering Enquirers, and old[5] in those singularities, we expect such Descriptions. Wherein[6] England is now so exact, that it yeelds not to other Countreys.

We pretend not to multiply vegetable divisions by Quincuncial and Reticulate plants; or erect a new Phytology. The Field of knowledge hath been so traced, it is hard to spring any thing new. Of old things we write something new, If truth may receive addition, or envy will have any thing new; since the Ancients knew the late Anatomicall discoveries, and Hippocrates the Circulation.

You have been so long out of trite learning, that 'tis hard to finde a subject proper for you; and if you have met with a Sheet upon this, we have missed our intention. In this multiplicity of writing, bye and barren Themes are best fitted for invention; Subjects so often discoursed confine the Imagination, and fix our conceptions unto the notions of fore-writers. Beside, such Discourses allow excursions, and venially admit of collaterall truths, though at some distance from their principals. Wherein if we sometimes take wide liberty, we are not single, but erre by great example.[7]

He that will illustrate the excellency of this order, may easily fail upon so spruce a Subject, wherein we have not affrighted the common Reader with any other Diagramms, then of it self; and have industriously declined illustrations from rare and unknown plants.

Your discerning judgement so well acquainted with that study, will expect herein no mathematicall truths, as well understanding how few generalities and U finita's[8] there are in nature. How Scaliger hath found exceptions in most Universals of Aristotle and Theophrastus. How Botanicall Maximes must have fair allowance, and are tolerably currant, if not intolerably over-ballanced by exceptions.

You have wisely ordered your vegetable delights, beyond the reach of exception.

The Turks who passt their dayes in Gardens here, will have Gardens also hereafter, and delighting in Flowers on earth, must have Lilies and Roses in Heaven. In Garden Delights 'tis not easie to hold a Mediocrity; that insinuating pleasure is seldome without some extremity. The Antients venially delighted in flourishing Gardens; Many were Florists that knew not the true use of a Flower; and in Plinies dayes none had directly treated of that Subject. Some commendably affected Plantations of venemous Vegetables, some confined their delights unto single plants, and Cato seemed to dote upon Cabbadge; While the Ingenuous delight of Tulipists, stands saluted with hard language, even by their own Professors.[9]

That in this Garden Discourse, we range into extraneous things, and many parts of Art and Nature, we follow herein the example of old and new Plantations, wherein noble spirits contented not themselves with Trees, but by the attendance of Aviaries, Fish Ponds, and all variety of Animals, they made their gardens the Epitome of the earth, and some resemblance of the secular shows of old.

That we conjoyn these parts of different Subjects,[10] or that this should succeed the other; Your judgement will admit without impute of incongruity; Since the delightfull World comes after death, and Paradise succeeds the Grave. Since the verdant state of things is the Symbole of the Resurrection, and to flourish in the state of Glory, we must first be sown in corruption. Beside the antient practise of Noble Persons, to conclude in Garden-Graves, and Urnes themselves of old, to be wrapt up in flowers and garlands.

Nullum sine venia placuisse eloquium,[11] is more sensibly understood by Writers, then by Readers; nor well apprehended by either, till works have hanged out like Apelles his Pictures; wherein even common eyes will finde something for emendation.

To wish all Readers of your abilities, were unreasonably to multiply the number of Scholars beyond the temper of these times. But unto this ill-judging age, we charitably desire a portion of your equity, judgement, candour, and ingenuity; wherein you are so rich, as not to lose by diffusion. And being a flourishing branch of that Noble Family,[12] unto which we owe so much observance, you are not new set, but long rooted in such perfections; whereof having had so lasting confirmation in your worthy conversation, constant amity, and expression; and knowing you such a serious Student in the highest arcana's of Nature; with much excuse we bring these low delights, and poor maniples to your Treasure.

Norwich May 1.

Your affectionate Friend,
and Servant,
THOMAS BROWNE.

Introduction

That Vulcan gave arrows unto Apollo and Diana the fourth day after their Nativities, according to Gentile Theology, may passe for no blinde apprehension of the Creation of the Sunne and Moon, in the work of the fourth day; When the diffused light contracted into Orbes, and shooting rayes, of those Luminaries. Plainer Descriptions there are from Pagan pens, of the creatures of the fourth day; While the divine Philosopher[1] unhappily omitteth the noblest part of the third; And Ovid (whom many conceive to have borrowed his description from Moses) coldly deserting the remarkable account of the text, in three words,[2] describeth this work of the third day; the vegetable creation, and first ornamentall Scene of nature; the primitive food of animals, and first story of Physick, in Dietetical conservation.

For though Physick may pleade high, from that medicall act of God, in casting so deep a sleep upon our first Parent; And Chirurgery[3] finde its whole art, in that one passage concerning the Rib of Adam, yet is there no rivality with Garden contrivance and Herbery. For if Paradise were planted the third day of the Creation, as wiser Divinity concludeth, the Nativity thereof was too early for Horoscopie; Gardens were before Gardiners, and but some hours after the earth.

Of deeper doubt is its Topography, and locall designation, yet being the primitive garden, and without much[4] controversie seated in the East; it is more then probable the first curiosity, and cultivation of plants, most flourished in those quarters. And since the Ark of Noah first toucht upon some mountains of Armenia, the planting art arose again in the East, and found its revolution not far from the place of its Nativity, about the Plains of those Regions. And if Zoroaster were either Cham, Chus, or Mizraim, they were early proficients therein, who left (as Pliny delivereth) a work of Agriculture.

However the account of the Pensill or hanging gardens of Babylon, if made by Semiramis, the third or fourth from Nimrod, is of no slender antiquity; which being not framed upon ordinary levell of ground, but raised upon pillars, admitting under-passages, we cannot accept as the first Babylonian Gardens; But a more eminent progress and advancement in that art, then any that went before it: Somewhat answering or hinting the old Opinion concerning Paradise it self, with many conceptions elevated, above the plane of the Earth.[5]

Nebuchodnosor whom some will have to be the famous Syrian king of Diodorus, beautifully repaired that City; and so magnificently built his[6] hanging gardens; that from succeeding Writers he had the honour of the first. From whence over-looking Babylon, and all the region about it, he found no circumscription to the eye of his ambition, till over-delighted with the bravery of this Paradise; in his melancholy metamorphosis, he found the folly of that delight, and a proper punishment in the contrary habitation, in wilde plantations and wanderings of the fields.

The Persian Gallants who destroyed this Monarchy, maintained their Botanicall bravery. Unto whom we owe the very name of Paradise; wherewith we meet not in Scripture before the time of Solomon, and conceived originally Persian. The word for that disputed Garden, expressing in the Hebrew no more then a Field enclosed, which from the same Root is content to derive a garden and a Buckler.

Cyrus the elder brought up in Woods and Mountains, when time and power enabled, pursued the dictate of his education, and brought the treasures of the field into rule and circumscription. So nobly beautifying the hanging Gardens of Babylon, that he was also thought to be the authour thereof.

Ahasuerus (whom many conceive to have been Artaxerxes Longimanus) in the Countrey and City of Flowers,[7] and in an open Garden, entertained his Princes and people, while Vashti more modestly treated the Ladies within the Palace thereof.

But if (as some opinion)[8] King Ahasuerus were Artaxerxes Mnemnon, that found a life and reign answerable unto his great memory, our magnified Cyrus was his second Brother; who gave the occasion of that memorable work, and almost miraculous retrait of Xenophon. A person of high spirit and honour, naturally a King, though fatally prevented by the harmlesse chance of *post*-geniture: Not only a Lord of Gardens, but a manuall planter thereof: disposing his trees like his armies in regular ordination. So that while old Laertas hath found a name in Homer for pruning hedges, and clearing away thorns and bryars; while King Attalus lives for his poysonous plantations of *Aconites*, Henbane, Hellebore, and plants hardly admitted within the walls of Paradise; While many of the Ancients do poorly live in the single names of Vegetables; All stories do look upon Cyrus, as the splendid and regular planter.

According whereto Xenophon[9] describeth his gallant plantation at Sardis, thus rendred by Strebæus. *Arbores pari intervallo sitas, rectos ordines, & omnia perpulchre in Quincuncem directa.*[10] Which we shall take for granted as being accordingly rendred by the most elegant of the Latines;[11] and by no made term, but in use before by Varro. That is the rows and orders so handsomely disposed; or five trees so set together, that a regular angularity, and through prospect, was left on every side, Owing this name not only unto the Quintuple number of Trees, but the figure declaring that number, which being doubled at the angle, makes up the Letter χ, that is the Emphaticall decussation, or fundamentall figure.

Now though in some ancient and modern practice the area or decussated plot, might be a perfect square, answerable to a *Tuscan Pedestall*, and the *Quinquernio* or Cinque-point of a dye; wherein by Diagonall lines the intersection was rectangular; accomodable unto Plantations of large growing Trees; and we must not deny our selves the advantage of this order; yet shall we chiefly insist upon that of Curtius and Porta,[12] in their brief description hereof. Wherein the *decussis* is made within a longilaterall square, with opposite angles, acute and obtuse at the intersection; and so upon progression making a Rhombus or Lozenge figuration, which seemeth very agreeable unto the Originall figure; Answerable whereunto we observe the decussated characters in many consulary Coynes, and even in those of Constantine and his Sons, which pretend their pattern in the Sky; the crucigerous Ensigne carried this figure, not transversly or rectangularly intersected, but in a decussation, after the form of an Andrean or Burgundian cross, which answereth this description.

Where by the way we shall decline the old Theme, so traced by antiquity of crosses and crucifixion: Whereof some being right, and of one single peece without traversion or transome, do little advantage our subject. Nor shall we take in the mysticall *Tau*, or the Crosse of our blessed Saviour, which having in some descriptions an *Empedon* or crossing foot-stay, made not one single transversion. And since the Learned Lipsius hath made some doubt even of the Crosse of St Andrew, since some Martyrologicall Histories deliver his death by the generall Name of a crosse, and Hippolitus will have him suffer by the sword; we should have enough to make out the received Crosse of that Martyr. Nor shall we urge the *labarum*, and famous Standard of Constantine, or make further use thereof, then as the first Letters in the Name of our Saviour Christ, in use among Christians, before the dayes of Constantine, to be observed in Sepulchral Monuments of Martyrs,[13] in the reign of Adrian, and Antoninus; and to be found in the Antiquities of the Gentiles, before the advent of Christ, as in the Medall of King Ptolomy, signed with the same characters, and might be the beginning of some word or name, which Antiquaries have not hit on.

We will not revive the mysterious crosses of Ægypt, with circles on their heads, in the breast of Serapis, and the hands of their Geniall spirits, not unlike the characters of Venus, and looked on by ancient Christians, with relation unto Christ. Since however they first began, the Ægyptians thereby expressed the processe and motion of the spirit of the world, and the diffusion thereof upon the Celestiall and Elementall nature; implyed by a circle and right-lined intersection. A secret in their Telesmes and magicall Characters among them. Though he that considereth the plain crosse[14] upon the head of the Owl in the Laterane Obelisk, or the crosse[15] erected upon a picher diffusing streams of water into two basins, with sprinkling branches in them, and all described upon a two-footed Altar, as in the Hieroglyphics of the brasen Table of Bembus; will hardly decline all thought of Christian signality in them.

We shall not call in the Hebrew *Tenupha*, or ceremony of their Oblations, waved by the Priest unto the four quarters of the world, after the form of a cross; as in the peace-offerings. And if it were clearly made out what is remarkably delivered from the Traditions of the Rabbins, that as the Oyle was powred coronally or circularlly upon the head of Kings, so the High-Priest was anointed decussatively or in the form of a X; though it could not escape a typicall thought of Christ, from mysticall considerators; yet being the conceit is Hebrew, we should rather expect its verification from Analogy in that language, then to confine the same unto the unconcerned Letters of Greece, or make it out by the characters of Cadmus or Palamedes.

Of this Quincunciall Ordination the Ancients practised much discoursed little; and the Moderns have nothing enlarged; which he that more nearly considereth, in the form of its square Rhombus, and decussation, with the several commodities, mysteries, parallelismes, and resemblances, both in Art and Nature, shall easily discern the elegancy of this order.

That this was in some wayes of practice in diverse and distant nations, hints or deliveries there are from no slender Antiquity. In the hanging Gardens of Babylon, from Abydenus, Eusebius, and others, Curtius describeth this Rule of decussation.[16] In the memorable garden of Alcinous anciently conceived an originall phancy, from Paradise, mention there is of well contrived order; For so hath Didymus and Eustachius expounded the emphatical word. Diomedes describing the Rurall possessions of his father, gives account in the same Language of Trees orderly planted. And Ulysses being a boy was promised by his Father fourty Figge-trees, and fifty rows of Vines producing all kinde of grapes.[17]

That the Eastern Inhabitants of India, made use of such order, even in open Plantations, is deducible from Theophrastus; who describing the trees whereof they made their garments, plainly delivereth that they were planted κατ᾿ ὄρχους, ('*in rows*') and in such order that at a distance men would mistake them for Vineyards. The same seems confirmed in Greece from a singular expression in Aristotle[18] concerning the order of Vines, delivered by a military term representing the orders of Souldiers, which also confirmeth the antiquity of this form yet used in vineall plantations.

That the same was used in Latine plantations is plainly confirmed from the commending penne of Varro, Quintilian, and handsome Description of Virgil.

> *Indulge ordinibus, nec secius omnis in unguem*
> *Arboribus positis, secto via limite quadret.*   Georg. 2

That the first plantations not long after the Floud were disposed after this manner, the generality and antiquity of this order observed in Vineyards, and Wine plantations, affordeth some conjecture. And since from judicious enquiry, Saturn who divided the world between his three sonnes, who beareth a Sickle in his hand, who taught the plantations of Vines, the setting, grafting of trees, and the best part of Agriculture, is discovered to be Noah, whether this early dispersed Husbandry in Vineyards, had not its Originall in that Patriarch, is no such Paralogicall doubt.

And if it were clear that this was used by Noah after the Floud, I could easily beleeve it was in use before it; Not willing to fix such ancient inventions no higher originall then Noah; Nor readily conceiving those aged Heroes, whose diet was vegetable, and only, or chiefly consisted in the fruits of the earth, were much deficient in their splendid cultivations; or after the experience of fifteen hundred years, left much for future discovery in Botanicall Agriculture. Nor fully perswaded that Wine was the invention of Noah, that fermented Liquors, which often make themselves, so long escaped their Luxury or experience; that the first sinne of the new world was no sin of the old. That Cain and Abel were the first that offered Sacrifice; or because the Scripture is silent that Adam or Isaac offered none at all.

Whether Abraham brought up in the first planting Countrey, observed not some rule hereof, when he planted a grove at Beer-sheba; or whether at least a like ordination were not in the Garden of Solomon, probability may contest. Answerably unto the wisedom of that eminent Botanologer, and orderly disposer of all his other works. Especially since this was one peece of Gallantry, wherein he pursued the specious part of felicity, according to his own description. *I made me Gardens and Orchards, and planted Trees in them of all kindes of fruit. I made me Pools of water, to water therewith the wood that bringeth forth Trees,*(Eccles. ii. 5,6) which was no ordinary plantation, if according to the *Targum*, or Chaldee Paraphrase, it contained all kindes of Plants, and some fetched as far as India; And the extent thereof were from the wall of Jerusalem unto the water of Siloah.

And if Jordan were but Jaar Eden, that is, the River of Eden, Genesar but Gansar or the Prince of Gardens; and it could be made out, that the Plain of Jordan were watered not comparatively, but causally, and because it was the Paradise of God, as the Learned Abramas[19] hinteth, he was not far from the Prototype and originall of Plantations. And since even in Paradise it self, the tree of knowledge was placed in the middle of the Garden, whatever was the ambient figure, there wanted not a centre and rule of decussation. Whether the groves and sacred Plantations of Antiquity, were not thus orderly placed, either by *quaternio's*, or quintuple ordinations, may favourably be doubted. For since they were so methodicall in the constitutions of their temples, as to observe the due scituation, aspect, manner, form, and order in Architectonicall relations, whether they were not as distinct in their groves and Plantations about them, in form and *species* respectively unto their Deities, is not without probability of conjecture. And in their groves of the Sunne this was a fit number, by multiplication to denote the dayes of the year; and might Hieroglyphically speak as much, as the mysticall *Statua* of Janus[20] in the Language of his fingers. And since they were so criticall in the number of his horses, the strings of his Harp, and rayes about his head, denoting the orbes of heaven, the Seasons and Moneths of the Yeare; witty Idolatry would hardly be flat in other appropriations.

CHAPTER II
The Quincunx Artificially Considered

Nor was this only a form of practise in Plantations, but found imitation from high Antiquity, in sundry artificiall contrivances and manuall operations. For to omit the position of squared stones, *cuneatim* or wedgwise in the Walls of Roman and Gothick buildings; and the *lithostrata* or figured pavements of the ancients, which consisted not all of square stones, but were divided into triquetrous segments, honey-combs, and sexangular figures, according to Vitruvius; The squared stones and bricks in ancient fabricks, were placed after this order. And two above or below conjoyned by a middle stone or Plinthus, observable in the ruines of Forum Nervæ, the Mausoleum of Augustus, the Pyramid of Cestius, and the sculpture draughts of the larger Pyramids of Ægypt. And therefore in the draughts of eminent fabricks, Painters do commonly imitate this order in the lines of their description.

In the Laureat draughts of sculpture and picture, the leaves and foliate works are commonly thus contrived, which is but in imitation of the *Pulvinaria*, and ancient pillow-work, observable in Ionick peeces, about columns, temples and altars. To omit many other analogies, in Architectonicall draughts, which art it self is founded upon fives,[1] as having its subject, and most gracefull peeces divided by this number.

The Triumphal Oval, and Civicall Crowns of Laurel, Oake, and Myrtle, when fully made, were pleated after this order. And to omit the crossed Crowns of Christian Princes; what figure that was which Anastatius described upon the head of Leo the third; or who first brought in the Arched Crown; That of Charles the great, (which seems the first remarkably closed Crown,) was framed after this manner;[2] with an intersection in the middle from the main crossing barres, and the interspaces, unto the frontal circle, continued by handsome network-plates, much after this order. Whereon we shall not insist, because from greater Antiquity, and practice of consecration, we meet with the radiated, and starry Crown, upon the head of Augustus, and many succeeding Emperors. Since the Armenians and Parthians had a peculiar royall Capp; and the Grecians from Alexander another kinde of diadem. And even Diadems themselves were but fasciations, and handsome ligatures, about the heads of Princes; nor wholly omitted in the mitrall Crown, which common picture seems to set too upright and forward upon the head of Aaron: Worne sometimes singly, or doubly by Princes, according to their Kingdomes; and no more to be expected from two Crowns at once, upon the head of Ptolomy.[3] And so easily made out when historians tell us, some bound up wounds, some hanged themselves with diadems.

The beds of the antients were corded somewhat after this fashion: That is not directly, as ours at present, but obliquely, from side to side, and after the manner of network; whereby they strengthened the spondæ or bedsides, and spent less cord in the work: as is demonstrated by Blancanus.[4]

And as they lay in crossed beds, so they sat upon seeming crosselegg'd seats: in which form the noblest thereof were framed: Observable in the triumphall seats, the *sella curulis*, or *Ædyle Chayres*, in the coyns of Cestius, Sylla, and Julius. That they sat also crosse legg'd many noble draughts declare; and in this figure the sitting gods and goddesses are drawn in medalls and medallions. And beside this kinde of work in Retiarie and hanging textures, in embroderies, and eminent needle-works; the like is obvious unto every eye in glass-windows. Nor only in Glassie contrivances, but also in Lattice and Stone-work, conceived in the Temple of Solomon; wherein the windows are termed *fenestræ reticulatæ*,[5] or lights framed like nets. And agreeable unto the Greek expression concerning Christ in the Canticles, looking through the nets,which ours hath rendered, *he looketh forth at the windows*, (Cant. ii. 9) shewing himselfe through the lattesse; that is, partly seen and unseen, according to the visible and invisible side of his nature. To omit the noble reticulate work, in the chapiters of the pillars of Solomon, with Lillies, and Pomegranats upon a network ground; and the *Craticula* or grate through which the ashes fell in the altar of burnt offerings.

That the networks and nets of antiquity were little different in the form from ours at present, is confirmable from the nets in the hands of the Retiarie gladiators, the proper combatants with the secutores. To omit the Conopeion or gnatnet, of the Ægyptians, the inventors of that Artifice: the rushey labyrinths of Theocritus; the nosegaynets, which hung from the head under the nostrils of Princes; and that uneasie metaphor of *Reticulum Jecoris*, which some expound the lobe, we the caule above the liver.[6] As for the famous network of Vulcan, which inclosed Mars and Venus, and caused that inextinguishable laugh in heaven;[7] since the gods themselves could not discern it, we shall not prie into it; Although why Vulcan bound them, Neptune loosed them, and Apollo should first discover them, might afford no vulgar mythologie. Heralds have not omitted this order or imitation thereof, while they Symbollically adorn their Scuchions with Mascles Fusils and Saltyrs, and while they disposed the figures of Ermins, and vaired coats in this Quincuncial method.[8]

The same is not forgot by Lapidaries while they cut their gemms pyramidally, or by æquicrural triangles. Perspective pictures, in their Base, Horison, and lines of distances, cannot escape these Rhomboidall decussations. Sculptors in their strongest shadows, after this order do draw their double Haches. And the very Americans do naturally fall upon it, in their neat and curious textures, which is also observed in the elegant artifices of Europe. But this is no law unto the woof of the neat *Retiarie* Spider, which seems to weave without transversion, and by the union of right lines to make out a continued surface, which is beyond the common art of Textury, and may still nettle Minerva[9] the Goddesse of that mystery. And he that shall hatch the little seeds, either found in small webs, or white round Egges, carried under the bellies of some Spiders, and behold how at their first production in boxes, they will presently fill the same with their webbs, may observe the early, and untaught finger of nature, and how they are natively provided with a stock, sufficient for such Texture.

The Rurall charm against Dodder, Tetter, and strangling weeds, was contrived after this order, while they placed a chalked Tile at the four corners, and one in the middle of their fields, which though ridiculous in the intention, was rationall in the contrivance, and a good way to diffuse the magick through all parts of the Area.

Somewhat after this manner they ordered the little stones in the old game of *Pentalithismus*, or casting up five stones to catch them on the back of their hand. And with some resemblance hereof, the *Proci* or Prodigall Paramours disposed their men, when they played at Penelope.[10] For being themselves an hundred and eight, they set fifty four stones on either side, and one in the middle, which they called Penelope, which he that hit was master of the game.

In Chesse-boards and Tables we yet finde Pyramids and Squares, I wish we had their true and ancient description, farre different from ours, or the *Chet mat* of the Persians, and might continue some elegant remarkables, as being an invention as High as Hermes the Secretary of Osyris,[11] figuring the whole world, the motion of the Planets, with Eclipses of Sunne and Moon.

Physicians are not without the use of this decussation in severall operations, in ligatures and union of dissolved continuities. Mechanicks make use hereof in forcipall Organs, and Instruments of Incision; wherein who can but magnifie the power of decussation, inservient to contrary ends, solution and consolidation, union, and division, illustrable from Aristotle in the old *Nucifragium* or Nutcracker, and the Instruments of Evulsion, compression or incision; which consisting of two *Vectes* or armes, converted towards each other, the innitency and stresse being made upon the *hypomochlion* or fulciment in the decussation, the greater compression is made by the union of two impulsors.

The Roman *Battalia*[12] was ordered after this manner, whereof as sufficiently known Virgil hath left but an hint, and obscure intimation. For thus were the maniples and cohorts of the *Hastati, Principes* and *Triarii* placed in their bodies, wherein consisted the strength of the Roman battle. By this Ordination they readily fell into each other; the Hastati being pressed, handsomely retired into the intervalls of the Principes, these into that of the Triarii, which making as it were a new body, might joyntly renew the battle, wherein consisted the secret of their successes.

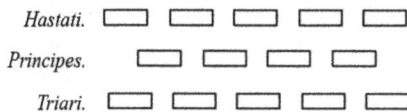

Hastati.   ▭   ▭   ▭   ▭   ▭

Principes.   ▭   ▭   ▭   ▭

Triari.   ▭   ▭   ▭   ▭   ▭

And therefore it was remarkably singular[13] in the battle of Africa, that Scipio fearing a rout from the Elephants of the Enemy, left not the Principes in their alternate distances, whereby the Elephants passing the vacuities of the Hastati, might have run upon them, but drew his battle into right order, and leaving the passages bare, defeated the mischief intended by the Elephants. Out of this figure were made too remarkable forms of Battle, the *Cuneus* and *Forceps*, or the sheare and wedge battles, each made of half a Rhombus, and but differenced by position. The wedge invented to break or work into a body, the forceps to environ and defeat the power thereof, composed out of the selectest Souldiery and disposed into the form of an V, wherein receiving the wedge, it inclosed it on both sides. After this form the famous Nasses[14] ordered his battle against the Franks, and by this figure the Almans were enclosed, and cut in peeces.

The Rhombus or Lozenge figure so visible in this order, was also a remarkable form of battle in the Grecian Cavalry,[15] observed by the Thessalians, and Philip King of Macedon, and frequently by the Parthians, As being most ready to turn every way, and best to be commanded, as having its ductors, or Commanders at each Angle.

The Macedonian *Phalanx* (a long time thought invincible) consisted of a long square. For though they might be sixteen in Rank and file, yet when they shut close, so that the sixt pike advanced before the first, though the number might be square, the figure was oblong, answerable unto the Quincunciall quadrate of Curtius. According to this square Thucydides delivers, the Athenians disposed their battle against the Lacedemonians brickwise,[16] and by the same word the Learned Guellius expoundeth the quadrate of Virgil, after the form of a brick or tile.

Secto via limite quadret. Com. in Virgil [Georgics, II, 278].

And as the first station and position of trees, so was the first habitation of men, not in round Cities, as of later foundation; For the form of Babylon the first City was square, and so shall also be the last, according to the description of the holy City in the Apocalyps. The famous pillars of Seth before the floud, had also the like foundation, if they were but antidiluvian Obelisks, and such as Cham and his Ægyptian race, imitated after the Floud.

But Nineveh which Authours acknowledge to have exceeded Babylon, was of a longilaterall figure,[17] ninety five Furlongs broad, and an hundred and fifty long, and so making about sixty miles in circuit, which is the measure of three dayes journey, according unto military marches, or castrensiall mansions. So that if Jonas entred at the narrower side, he found enough for one dayes walk to attain the heart of the City, to make his Proclamation. And if we imagine a City extending from Ware to London, the expression will be moderate of six score thousand Infants, although we allow vacuities, fields, and intervals of habitation as there needs must be when the monument of Ninus took up no lesse then ten furlongs.

And, though none of the seven wonders, yet a noble peece of Antiquity, and made by a Copy exceeding all the rest, had its principall parts disposed after this manner, that is, the Labyrinth of Crete, built upon a long quadrate, containing five large squares, communicating by right inflections, terminating in the centre of the middle square, and lodging of the *Minotaur*, if we conform unto the description of the elegant medall thereof in Agostino.[18] And though in many accounts we reckon grosly by the square, yet is that very often to be accepted as a long sided quadrate, which was the figure of the Ark of the Covenant, the table of the Shew-bread, and the stone wherein the names of the twelve Tribes were engraved, that is, three in a row, naturally making a longilaterall Figure, the perfect quadrate being made by nine.

What figure the stones themselves maintained, tradition and Scripture are silent, yet Lapidaries in precious stones affect a Table or long square, and in such proportion, that the two laterall, and also the three inferiour Tables are equall unto the superiour, and the angles of the laterall Tables, contain and constitute the *hypothenusæ*, or broader sides subtending.

That the Table of the Law were of this figure, general imitation and tradition hath confirmed; yet are we unwilling to load the shoulders of Moses with such massie stones, as some pictures lay upon them, since 'tis plainly delivered that he came down with them in his hand; since the word strictly taken implies no such massie hewing, but cutting, and fashioning of them into shape and surface; since some will have them Emeralds, and if they were made of the materials of Mount Sina, not improbable that they were marble; Since the words were not many, the letters short of seven hundred, and the Tables written on both sides required no such capacity.

The beds of the Ancients were different from ours at present, which are almost square, being framed oblong, and about a double unto their breadth; not much unlike the *area*, or bed of this Quincuncial quadrate. The single beds of Greece were six foot,[19] and a little more in length, three in breadth; the Giant-like bed of Og, which had four cubits of bredth, nine and a half in length, varied not much from this proportion. The Funeral bed of King Cheops, in the greater Pyramid, which holds seven in length, and four foot in bredth, had no great difformity from this measure; And whatsoever were the bredth, the length could hardly be lesse, of the tyrannical bed of Procrustes, since in a shorter measure he had not been fitted with persons for his cruelty of extension. But the old sepulchral bed, or Amazonian Tomb in the market-place of Megara,[20] was in the form of a Lozenge; readily made out by the composure of the body. For the arms not lying fasciated or wrapt up after the Grecian manner, but in a middle distention, the including lines will strictly make out that figure.

CHAPTER III
The Quincunx Naturally Considered

Now although this elegant ordination of vegetables, hath found coincidence or imitation in sundry works of Art, yet is it not also destitute of naturall examples, and though overlooked by all, was elegantly observable, in severall works of nature.

Could we satisfie ourselves in the position of the lights above, or discover the wisedom of that order so invariably maintained in the fixed Stars of heaven; Could we have any light, why the stellary part of the first masse, separated into this order, that the Girdle of Orion should ever maintain its line, and the two Starres in Charles's Wain never leave pointing at the Pole-Starre, we might abate the Pythagoricall Musick of the Spheres, the sevenfold Pipe of Pan; and the strange Cryptography of Gaffarell in his Starrie Booke of Heaven.

But not to look so high as Heaven or the single Quincunx of the Hyades upon the head of Taurus, the Triangle, and remarkable Crusero about the foot of the Centaur; observable rudiments there are hereof in subterraneous concretions, and bodies in the Earth; in the Gypsum or *Talcum Rhomboides*, in the Favaginites or honey-comb-stone, in the *Asteria* and *Astroites*, and in the crucigerous stone of S. Iago of Gallicia.

The same is observably effected in the Julus, Catkins, or pendulous excrescencies of severall Trees, of Wallnuts, Alders, and Hazels, which hanging all the Winter, and maintaining their Net-worke close, by the expansion thereof are the early foretellers of the Spring, discoverable also in long Pepper, and elegantly in the Julus of *Calamus Aromaticus*,[1] so plentifully growing with us in the first palmes of Willowes, and in the Flowers of Sycamore, Petasites, Asphodelus, and *Blattaria*, before explication. After such order stand the flowery Branches in our best spread Verbascum, and the seeds about the spicous head or torch of *Tapsas Barbatus*, in as fair a regularity as the circular and wreathed order will admit, which advanceth one side of the square, and makes the same Rhomboidall.

In the squamous heads of Scabious, Knapweed, and the elegant *Jacea Pinea*, and in the Scaly composure of the Oak-Rose, which some years most aboundeth. After this order hath Nature planted the Leaves in the Head of the common and prickled Artichoak; wherein the black and shining Flies do shelter themselves, when they retire from the purple Flower about it; The same is also found in the pricks, sockets, and impressions of the seeds, in the pulp or bottome thereof; wherein do elegantly stick the Fathers of their Mother.[2] To omit the Quincunciall Specks on the top of the Miscle-berry, especially that which grows upon the *Tilia* or Lime-Tree. And the remarkable disposure of those yellow fringes about the purple Pestill of Aaron, and elegant clusters of Dragons, so peculiarly secured by nature, with an umbrella or skreening Leaf about them.[3]

The Spongy leaves of some Sea-wracks, Fucus, Oaks, in their severall kindes, found about the Shoar, with ejectments of the Sea, are over-wrought with Net-work elegantly containing this Order,[4] which plainly declareth the naturality of this texture; And how the needle of nature delighteth to work, even in low and doubtful vegetations.

The *Arbustetum* or Thicket on the head of the Teazell, may be observed in this order: And he that considereth that fabrick so regularly palisadoed, and stemm'd with flowers of the royall colour; in the house of the solitary maggot,[5] may finde the Seraglio of Solomon, And contemplating the calicular shafts, and uncous disposure of their extremities, so accommodable unto the office of abstersion, not condemne as wholly improbable the conceit of those who accept it, for the herbe *Borith*. (Jer. ii. 22) Where by the way, we could with much inquiry never discover any transfiguration, in this abstemious insect, although we have kept them long in their proper houses, and boxes. Where some wrapt up in their webbs, have lived upon their own bowels, from September unto July.

In such a grove doe walke the little creepers about the head of the burre. And such an order is observed in the aculeous prickly plantation, upon the heads of several common thistles, remarkably in the notable palisadoes about the flower of the milk-thistle; and he that inquireth into the little bottome of the globe-thistle, may finde that gallant bush arise from a scalpe of like disposure.

The white umbrella or medicall bush of Elder, is an Epitome of this order: arising from five main stemms Quincuncially disposed, and tollerably maintained in their subdivisions. To omit the lower observations in the seminal spike of Mercurie, weld, and Plantane.

Thus hath nature ranged the flowers of Santfoyne, and French honey suckle; and somewhat after this manner hath ordered the bush in Jupiters beard, or houseleek; which old superstition set on the tops of houses, as a defensative against lightening, and thunder. The like in Fenny Seagreen or the water Souldier;[6] which, though a militarie name from Greece, makes out the Roman order.

A like ordination there is in the favaginous[7] Sockets, and Lozenge seeds of the noble flower of the Sunne. Wherein in Lozenge figured boxes nature shuts up the seeds, and balsame which is about them.

But the Firre and Pinetree from their fruits doe naturally dictate this position. The Rhomboidall protuberances in Pineapples maintaining this Quincuncial order unto each other, and each Rhombus in it selfe. Thus are also disposed the triangular foliations, in the conicall fruit of the firre tree, orderly shadowing and protecting the winged seeds below them.

The like so often occurreth to the curiosity of observers, especially in spicated seeds and flowers, that we shall not need to take in the single Quincunx of Fuchsius in the grouth of the masle fearn, the seedie disposure of Gramen

Ischemon, and the trunk or neat Reticulate work in the codde of the Sachell palme.

For even in very many round stalk plants, the leaves are set after a Quintuple ordination, the first leaf answering the fifth, in laterall disposition. Wherein the leaves successively rounding the stalke, in foure at the furthest the compass is absolved, and the fifth leafe or sprout, returns to the position of the other fift before it; as in accounting upward is often observable in furre pellitorye, Ragweed, the sproutes of Oaks, and thorns upon pollards, and very remarkably in the regular disposure of the rugged excrescencies in the yearly shoots of the Pine.

But in square stalked plants, the leaves stand respectively unto each other, either in crosse or decussation to those above or below them, arising at crosse positions; whereby they shadow not each other, and better resist the force of winds, which in a parallel situation, and upon square stalkes would more forcibly bear upon them.

And to omit, how leaves and sprouts, which compasse not the stalk, are often set in a Rhomboides, and making long, and short Diagonals, doe stand like the leggs of Quadrupeds when they goe: Nor to urge the thwart enclosure and furdling of flowers, and blossomes, before explication, as in the multiplyed leaves of Pionie; And the Chiasmus in five leaved flowers, while one lies wrapt about the staminous beards, the other foure obliquely shutting and closing upon each other; and how even flowers which consist of foure leaves, stand not ordinarily in three and one, but two, and two crossewise unto the Stylus; even the Autumnal budds, which awaite the returne of the sun, doe after the winter solstice multiply their calicular leaves, making little Rhombuses, and network figures, as in the Sycamore and Lilac.

The like is discoverable in the original production of plants, which first putting forth two leaves, those which succeed, bear not over each other, but shoot obliquely or crossewise, untill the stalke appeareth; which sendeth not forth its first leaves without all order unto them; and he that from hence can discover in what position the two first leaves did arise, is no ordinary observator.

Where by the way, he that observeth the rudimental spring of seeds, shall finde strict rule, although not after this order. How little is required unto effectual generation, and in what diminutives the plastick principle lodgeth, is exemplified in seeds, wherein the greater mass affords so little comproduction. In Beanes the leaf and root sprout from the Germen, the main sides split, and lye by, and in some pull'd up near the time of blooming, we have found the pulpous sides intire or little wasted. In Acorns the nebb dilating splitteth the two sides, which sometimes lye whole, when the Oak is sprouted two handfuls. In Lupins these pulpy sides do sometimes arise with the stalk in a resemblance of two fat leaves. Wheat and Rye will grow up, if after they have shot some tender Roots, the adhering pulp be taken from them. Beanes will prosper though a part be cut away, and so much set as sufficeth to contain and keep the Germen[16] close. From this superfluous pulp in unkindely, and wet years, may arise that multiplicity of little insects, which infest the Roots and Sprouts of tender Graines and pulses.

In the little nebbe or fructifying principle, the motion is regular, and not transvertible, as to make that ever the leaf, which nature intendeth the root; observable from their conversion, until they attain the right position, if seeds be set inversedly.

In vain we expect the production of plants from different parts of the seed, from the same *corculum* or little original proceed both germinations; and in the power of this slender particle lye many Roots, that though the same be pull'd away, the generative particle will renew them again, and proceed to a perfect plant; And malt may be observed to grow, though the Cummes be fallen from it.

The seminall nebbe hath a defined and single place, and not extended unto both extremes. And therefore many too vulgarly conceive that Barley and Oats grow at both ends; For they arise from one *punctilio* or generative nebbe, and the Speare sliding under the husk, first appeareth nigh the toppe. But in Wheat and Rye being bare the sprouts are seen together. If Barley unhulled would grow, both would appear at once. But in this and Oat-meal the nebbe is broken away, which makes them the milder food, and lesse apt to raise fermentation in Decoctions.

Men taking notice of what is outwardly visible, conceive a sensible priority in the Root. But as they begin from one part, so they seem to start and set out upon one signall of nature. In Beans yet soft, in Pease while they adhere unto the Cod, the rudimentall Leafe and Root are discoverable. In the seeds of Rocket and Mustard, sprouting in Glasses of water, when the one is manifest the other is also perceptible. In muddy waters apt to breed Duckweed, and Periwinkles, if the first and rudimentall stroaks of Duckweed be observed, the Leaves and Root anticipate not each other. But in the Date-stone the first sprout is neither root nor leaf distinctly, but both together; For the Germination being to passe through the Navell and hole about the midst of the stone, the generative germ is faine to enlengthen it self, and shooting out about an inch, at that distance divideth into the ascending and descending portion.

And though it be generally thought that Seeds will root at that end, where they adhere to their Originals, and observable it is that the nebbe sets most often next the stalk, as in Grains, Pulses, and most small Seeds, yet is it hardly made out in many greater plants. For in Acornes, Almonds, Pistachios, Wallnuts, and accuminated shells, the germ puts forth at the remotest part of the pulp. And therefore to set Seeds in that posture, wherein the Leaf and Roots may shoot right without contortion, or forced circumvolution, which might render them strongly rooted, and straighter, were a Criticisme in Agriculture. And nature seems to have made some provision hereof in many from their figure, that as they fall from the tree they may lye in Positions agreeable to such advantages.

Beside the open and visible Testicles of plants, the seminall pores lie in great part invisible, while the Sun findes polypody in stone-wals, the little stinging Nettle, and nightshade in barren sandy High-wayes, Scurvy-grasse in Greeneland, and unknown plants in earth brought from remote Countries. Beside the known longevity of some Trees, what is the most lasting herb, or seed, seems not easily determinable. Mandrakes upon known account have lived near an hundred yeares. Seeds found in Wilde-Fowls Gizards have sprouted in the earth. The Seeds of Marjorane and *Stramonium* carelesly kept, have grown after seven years. Even in Garden-plots long fallow, and digged up, the seeds of *Blattaria* and yellow henbane, after twelve years burial have produced themselves again.

That bodies are first spirits Paracelsus could affirm, which in the maturation of Seeds and fruits, seems obscurely implied by Aristotle,[8] when he delivereth, that the spirituous parts are converted into water, and the water into earth, and attested by observation in the maturative progresse of Seeds, wherein at first may be discerned a flatuous distension of the husk, afterwards a thin liquor, which longer time digesteth into a pulp or kernell observable in Almonds and large Nuts. And some way answered in the progressionall perfection of animall semination, in its spermaticall maturation, from crude pubescency unto perfection. And even that seeds themselves in their rudimentall discoveries, appear in foliaceous surcles, or sprouts within their coverings, in a diaphonous gellie, before deeper incrassation, is also visibly verified in Cherries, Acorns, Plums.

From seminall considerations, either in reference unto one mother, or distinction from animall production, the holy Scripture describeth the vegetable creation; And while it divideth plants but into Herb and Tree, though it seemeth to make but an accidental division, from magnitude, it tacitely containeth the naturall distinction of vegetables, observed by Herbarists, and comprehending the four kinds. For since the most naturall distinction is made from the production of leaf or stalk, and plants after the two first seminall leaves, do either proceed to send forth more leaves, or a stalk, and the folious and stalky emission distinguisheth herbs and trees, and stand Authentically differenced, but from the accidents of the stalk.

The Æquivocall production of things under undiscerned principles, makes a large part of generation, though they seem to hold a wide univocacy in their set and certain Originals, while almost every plant breeds its peculiar insect, most a Butterfly, moth or fly, wherein the Oak seems to contain the largest seminality, while the Julus,[9] Oak, apple, dill, woolly tuft, foraminous roundles upon the leaf, and grapes under ground make a Fly with some difference. The great variety of Flyes lyes in the variety of their originals, in the seeds of Caterpillars or Cankers there lyeth not only a Butterfly or Moth, but if they be sterill or untimely cast, their production is often a Fly, which we have also observed from corrupted and mouldred Egges, both of Hens and Fishes; To omit the generation of Bees out of the bodies of dead Heifers, or what is stranger yet well attested, the production of Eeles in the backs of living Cods and Perches.[10]

The exiguity and smallnesse of some seeds extending to large productions is one of the magnalities of nature, somewhat illustrating the work of the Creation, and vast production from nothing. The true seeds[11] of Cypresse and Rampions are indistinguishable by old eyes. Of the seeds of Tobacco a thousand make not one grain. The disputed seeds of Harts tongue, and Maidenhair, require a greater number. From such undiscernable seminalities arise spontaneous productions. He that would discern the rudimentall stroak of a plant, may behold it in the Originall of Duckweed, at the bignesse of a pins point, from convenient water in glasses, wherein a watchfull eye may also discover the puncticular Originals of Periwincles and Gnats.

That seeds of some Plants are lesse then any animals, seems of no clear decision; That the biggest of Vegetables exceedeth the biggest of Animals, in full bulk, and all dimensions, admits exception in the Whale, which in length and above ground measure, will also contend with tall Oakes. That the richest odour of plants, surpasseth that of Animals may seem of some doubt, since animall-musk, seems to excell the vegetable, and we finde so noble a scent in the Tulip-Fly, and Goat-Beetle.[12]

Now whether seminall nebbes hold any sure proportion unto seminall enclosures, why the form of the germe doth not answer the figure of the enclosing pulp, why the nebbe is seated upon the solid, and not the channeld side of the seed as in grains, why since we often meet with two yolks in one shell, and sometimes one Egge within another, we do not oftener meet with two nebbes in one distinct seed: why since the Egges of a Hen laid at one course, do commonly out-weigh the bird, and some moths coming out of their cases, without assistance of food, will lay so many Egges as to outweigh their bodies, trees rarely bear their fruit, in that gravity or proportion: Whether in the germination of seeds according to Hippocrates, the lighter part ascendeth, and maketh the sprout, the heaviest tending downward frameth the root; Since we observe that the first shoot of seeds in water, will sink or bow down at the upper and leafing end: Whether it be not more rational Epicurisme to contrive whole dishes out of the nebbes and spirited particles of plants, then from the Gallatures and treddles of Egges; since that part is found to hold no seminal share in Oval Generation, are quæries which might enlarge but must conclude this digression.

And though not in this order, yet how nature delighteth in this number, and what consent and coordination there is in the leaves and parts of flowers, it cannot escape our observation in no small number of plants. For the calicular or supporting and closing leaves, do answer the number of the flowers, especially in such as exceed not the number of Swallows Egges;[13] as in Violets, Stichwort, Blossomes, and flowers of one leaf have often five divisions, answered by a like number of calicular leaves; as *Gentianella, Convolvulus*, Bell-flowers. In many the flowers, blades, or staminous shootes and leaves are all equally five, as in cockle, mullein and *Blattaria*; Wherein the flowers before explication are pentagonally wrapped up, with some resemblance of the *blatta* or moth from whence it hath its name: But the contrivance of nature is singular in the opening and shutting of Bindeweeds, performed by five inflexures, distinguishable by pyramidicall figures, and also different colours.

The rose at first is thought to have been of five leaves, as it yet groweth wilde among us; but in the most luxuriant, the calicular leaves do still maintain that number. But nothing is more admired then the five Brethren of the Rose, and the strange disposure of the Appendices or Beards, in the calicular leaves thereof, which in despair of resolution is tolerably salved from this contrivance, best ordered and suited for the free closure of them before explication. For those two which are smooth, and of no beard are contrived to lye undermost, as without prominent parts, and fit to be smoothly covered; the other two which are beset with Beards on either side, stand outward and uncovered, but the fifth or half-bearded leaf is covered on the bare side but on the open side stands free, and bearded like the other.

Besides a large number of leaves have five divisions, and may be circumscribed by a *Pentagon* or figure of five Angles, made by right lines from the extremity of their leaves, as in Maple, Vine, Figge-Tree: But five-leaved flowers are commonly disposed circularly about the Stylus; according to the higher Geometry of nature, dividing a circle by five radii, which concurre not to make Diameters, as in Quadrilaterall and sexangular Intersections.

Now the number of five is remarkable in every circle, not only as the first sphærical number, but the measure of sphærical motion. For sphærical bodies move by fives, and every globular figure placed upon a plane, in direct volutation, returns to the first point of contaction in the fifth touch, accounting by the Axes of the Diameters or Cardinall points of the four quarters thereof. And before it arriveth unto the same point again, it maketh five circles equall unto it self, in each progresse from those quarters, absolving an equall circle.

By the same number doth nature divide the circle of the Sea-Starre, and in that order and number disposeth those elegant Semi-circles, or dentall sockets and egges in the Sea Hedge-hogge. And no mean Observations hereof there is in the Mathematicks of the neatest Retiary Spider, which concluding in fourty four Circles, from five Semidiameters beginneth that elegant texture.

And after this manner doth lay the foundation of the circular branches of the Oak, which being five-cornered, in the tender annual sprouts, and manifesting upon incision the signature of a Starre, is after made circular, and swel'd into a round body: Which practice of nature is become a point of art, and makes two Problemes in Euclide.[14] But the Bryar which sends forth shoots and prickles from its angles, maintains its pentagonnall figure, and the unobserved signature of a handsome porch within it. To omit the five small buttons dividing the Circle of the Ivy-berry, and the five characters in the Winter stalk of the Walnut, with many other Observables, which cannot escape the eyes of signal discerners; Such as know where to finde Ajax his name in *Gallitricum*, or Aarons Mitre in Henbane.

Quincuncial forms and ordinations, are also observable in animal figurations. For to omit the hioides or throat-bone of animals, the *furcula* or merry-thought in birds, which supporteth the *scapulæ*, affording a passage for the windepipe and the gullet, the wings of Flyes, and disposure of their legges in their first formation from maggots, and the position of their horns, wings and legges, in their Aurelian cases and swadling clouts: The back of the *Cimex Arboreus*, found often upon Trees and lesser plants, doth elegantly discover the Burgundian decussation; And the like is observable in the belly of the *Notonecton*, or water-Beetle, which swimmeth on its back, and the handsome Rhombusses of the Sea-poult, or Werrell, on either side the Spine.

The sexangular Cels in the Honeycombs of Bees, are disposeth after this order, much there is not of wonder in the confused Houses of Pismires, though much in their busie life and actions, more in the edificial Palaces of Bees and Monarchical spirits; who make their combs six-corner'd, declining a circle, whereof many stand not close together, and compleatly fill the area of the place; But rather affecting a six-sided figure, whereby every cell affords a common side unto six more, and also a fit receptacle for the Bee it self, which gathering into a Cylindrical Figure, aptly enters its sexangular house, more nearly approaching a circular Figure, then either doth the Square or Triangle. And the Combes themselves so regularly contrived, that their mutual intersections make three Lozenges at the bottome of every Cell; which severally regarded make three Rows of neat Rhomboidall Figures, connected at the angles, and so continue three several chains throughout the whole comb.

As for the *Favago* found commonly on the Sea shoar, though named from an honey-comb, it but rudely makes out the resemblance, and better agrees with the round Cels of humble Bees. He that would exactly discern the shop of a Bees mouth, need observing eyes, and good augmenting glasses; wherein is discoverable one of the neatest peeces in nature, and must have a more piercing eye then mine; who findes out the shape of Buls heads, in the guts of Drones pressed out behinde, according to the experiment of Gomesius;[15] wherein notwithstanding there seemeth somewhat which might incline a pliant fancy to credulity of similitude.

A resemblance hereof there is in the orderly and rarely disposed Cels, made by Flyes and Insects, which we have often found fastened about small sprigs, and in those cottonary and woolly pillows, which sometimes we meet with fastened unto Leaves, there is included an elegant Net-work Texture, out of which come many small Flies. And some resemblance there is of this order in the Egges of some Butterflies and moths, as they stick upon leaves, and other substances; which being dropped from behinde, nor directed by the eye, doth neatly declare how nature Geometrizeth, and observeth order in all things.

A like correspondency in figure is found in the skins and outward teguments of animals, whereof a regardable part are beautiful by this texture. As the backs of several Snakes and Serpents, elegantly remarkable in the *Aspis*, and the Dart-snake, in the Chiasmus and larger decussations upon the back of the Rattlesnake, and in the close and finer texture of the *Mater formicarum*, or snake that delights in Ant-hills; whereby upon approach of outward injuries, they can raise a thicker Phalanx on their backs, and handsomely contrive themselves into all kindes of flexures: Whereas their bellies are commonly covered with smooth semi-circular divisions, as best accommodable unto their quick and gliding motion.

This way is followed by nature in the peculiar and remarkable tayl of the Bever, wherein the scaly particles are disposed, somewhat after this order, which is the plainest resolution of the wonder of *Bellonius*, while he saith, with incredible Artifice hath Nature framed the tayl or Oar of the Bever: where by the way we cannot but wish a model of their houses, so much extolled by some Describers: wherein since they are so bold as to venture upon three stages, we might examine their Artifice in the contignations, the rule and order in the compartitions; or whether that magnified structure be any more then a rude rectangular pyle or meer hovell-building.

Thus works the hand of nature in the feathery plantation about birds. Observable in the skins of the breast,[16] legs and Pinions of Turkies, Geese, and Ducks, and the Oars or finny feet of Water-Fowl: And such a naturall Net is the scaly covering of Fishes, of Mullets, Carps, Tenches, &c. even in such as are excoriable and consist of smaller scales, as Bretts, Soals, and Flounders. The like Reticulate grain is observable in some Russia Leather. To omit the ruder Figures of the ostracion, the triangular or cunny fish, or the pricks of the Sea-Porcupine.

The same is also observable in some parts of the skin of man, in habits of neat textures, and therefore not unaptly compared unto a Net: We shall not affirm that from such grounds, the Ægyptian Embalmers imitated this texture. Yet in their linnen folds the same is still observable among their neatest Mummies, in the figures of Isis and Osyris, and the Tutelary spirits in the Bembine Table. Nor is it to be over-looked how Orus, the Hieroglyphick of the world is described in a Net-work covering, from the shoulder to the foot. And (not to enlarge upon the cruciated character of Trismegistus, or handed crosses,[17] so often occurring in the Needles of Pharaoh, and Obelisks of Antiquity) the *Statuæ Isiacæ*, Teraphims, and little Idols, found about the Mummies, do make a decussation or Jacobs Crosse, with their armes, like that on the head of Ephraim and Manasses, and this decussis is also graphically described between them.

This Reticulate or Net-work was also considerable in the inward parts of man, not only from the first *subtegmen* or warp of his formation, but in the netty fibres of the veins and vessels of life; wherein according to common Anatomy the right and transverse fibres are decussated, by the oblique fibres; and so must frame a Reticulate and Quincunciall Figure by their Obliquations, Emphatically extending that Elegant expression of Scripture, *Thou hast curiously embroydered me, thou hast wrought me up after the finest way of texture, and as it were with a Needle.*

Nor is the same observable only in some parts, but in the whole body of man, which upon the extension of arms and legges, doth make out a square, whose intersection is at the genitals. To omit the phantastical Quincunx, in Plato of the first Hermaphrodite or double man, united at the Loynes, which Jupiter after divided.

A rudimentall resemblance hereof there is in the cruciated and rugged folds of the *Reticulum*, or Net-like Ventricle of ruminating horned animals, which is the second in order, and culinarily called the Honey-comb. For many divisions there are in the stomack of severall animals; what number they maintain in the *Scarus* and ruminating Fish, common description, or our own experiment hath made no discovery. But in the Ventricle of Porpuses there are three divisions. In many Birds a crop, Gizard, and little receptacle before it; but in Cornigerous animals, which chew the cudd, there are no less then four of distinct position and office.[18]

The Reticulum by these crossed cels, makes a further digestion, in the dry and exuccous part of the Aliment received from the first Ventricle. For at the bottome of the gullet there is a double Orifice; What is first received at the mouth descendeth into the first and greater stomack, from whence it is returned into the mouth again; and after a fuller mastication, and salivous mixture, what part thereof descendeth again, in a moist and succulent body, it slides down the softer and more permeable Orifice, into the Omasus or third stomack; and from thence conveyed into the fourth, receives its last digestion. The other dry and exuccous part after rumination by the larger and stronger orifice beareth into the first stomack, from thence into the Reticulum, and so progressively into the other divisions. And therefore in Calves newly calved, there is little or no use of the two first Ventricles, for the milk and liquid aliment slippeth down the softer Orifice, into the third stomack; where making little or no stay, it passeth into the fourth, the seat of the *Coagulum*, or Runnet, or that division of stomack which seems to bear the name of the whole, in the Greek translation of the Priests Fee, in the Sacrifice of Peace-offerings. (Leviticus. 7. 31)

As for those Rhomboidal Figures made by the Cartilagineous parts of the Wezon, in the Lungs of great Fishes, and other animals, as Rondeletius discovered, we have not found them so to answer our figure as to be drawn into illustration; Something we expected in the more discernable texture of the lungs of frogs, which notwithstanding being but two curious bladders not weighing above a grain, we found interwoven with veins not observing any just order. More orderly situated are those cretaceous and chalky concretions found sometimes in the bignesse of a small fech on either side their spine; which being not agreeable unto our order, nor yet observed by any, we shall not here discourse on.

But had we found a better account and tolerable Anatomy, of that prominent jowle of the *Sperma Ceti* Whale,[19] then questuary operation, or the stench of the last cast upon our shoar, permitted, we might have perhaps discovered some handsome order in those Net-like seases and sockets, made like honey-combs, containing that medicall matter.

Lastly, The incession or locall motion of animals is made with analogy unto this figure, by decussative diametrals, Quincunciall Lines and angles. For to omit the enquiry how Butterflies and breezes move their four wings, how birds and fishes in ayre and water move by joynt stroaks of opposite wings and Finnes, and how salient animals in jumping forward seem to arise and fall upon a square base; As the station of most Quadrupeds, is made upon a long square, so in their motion they make a Rhomboides; their common progression being performed Diametrally, by decussation and crosse advancement of their legges, which not observed begot that remarkable absurdity in the position of the legges of Castors horse in the Capitol. The Snake which moveth circularly makes his spires in like order, the convex and concave spirals answering each other at alternate distances; In the motion of man the armes and legges observe this thwarting position, but the legges alone do move Quincuncially by single angles with some resemblance of an V measured by successive advancement from each foot, and the angle of indenture great or lesse, according to the extent or brevity of the stride.

Studious Observators may discover more analogies in the orderly book of nature, and cannot escape the Elegancy of her hand in other correspondencies. The Figures of nails and crucifying appurtenances, are but precariously made out in the *Granadilla* or flower of Christs passion: And we despair to behold in these parts that handsome draught of crucifixion in the fruit of the *Barbado* Pine. The seminal Spike of *Phalaris*, or great shaking grasse, more nearly answers the tayl of a Rattle-Snake, then many resemblances in Porta: And if the man Orchis[20] of Columna be well made out, it excelleth all analogies. In young Wallnuts cut athwart, it is not hard to apprehend strange characters; and in those of somewhat elder growth, handsome ornamental draughts about a plain crosse. In the root of Osmond or Water fern, every eye may discern the form of a Half Moon, Rainbow, or half the character of Pisces. Some finde Hebrew, Arabick, Greek, and Latine Characters in Plants; In a common one among us we seem to read, Acaia, Viviu, Lilil.

Right lines and circles make out the bulk of plants; In the parts thereof we finde Helicall or spirall roundles, voluta's, conicall Sections, circular Pyramids, and frustums of Archimedes; And cannot overlook the orderly hand of nature, in the alternate succession of the flat and narrower sides in the tender shoots of the Ashe, or the regular inequality of bignesse in the five-leaved flowers of Henbane, and something like in the calicular leaves of *Tutson*. How the spots of *Persicaria* do manifest themselves between the sixt and tenth ribbe. How the triangular capp in the stemme or stylus of Tuleps doth constantly point at three outward leaves. That spicated flowers do open first at the stalk. That white flowers have yellow thrums or knops. That the nebbe of Beans and Pease do all look downward, and so presse not upon each other; And how the seeds of many pappous or downy flowers lockt up in sockets after a gomphosis[21] or mortis-articulation, diffuse themselves circularly into branches of rare order, observable in *Tragopogon* or Goats-beard, conformable to the Spiders web, and the Radii in like manner telarely inter-woven.

And how in animall natures, even colours hold correspondencies, and mutuall correlations. That the colour of the Caterpillar will shew again in the Butterfly, with some latitude is allowable. Though the regular spots in their wings seem but a mealie adhesion, and such as may be wiped away, yet since they come in this variety, out of their cases, there must be regular pores in those parts and membranes, defining such Exudations.

That Augustus[22] had native notes on his body and belly, after the order and number in the Starre of *Charles Wayne*, will not seem strange unto astral Physiognomy, which accordingly considereth moles in the body of man, or Physicall Observators, who from the position of moles in the face, reduce them to rule and correspondency in other parts. Whether after the like method medicall conjecture may not be raised, upon parts inwardly affected; since parts about the lips are the critical seats of Pustules discharged in Agues; And scrophulous tumours about the neck do often speak the like about the Mesentery, may also be considered.

The russet neck to be observed in white yoiung lambs, which afterward vanisheth, seems but adventitious, and may owe its tincture to some contraction in the womb; But that if sheep have any black or deep russet in their faces, they want not the same about their legges and feet; That black Hounds have mealy mouths and feet; That black Cows which have any white in their tayls, should not misse of some in their bellies; and if all white in their bodies, yet if black-mouth'd, their ears and feet maintain the same colour, are correspondent tinctures not ordinarily failing in nature, which easily unites the accidents of extremities, since in some generations she transmutes the parts themselves, while in the *Aurelian Metamorphoses* the head of the canker becomes the Tayl of the Butterfly. Which is in some way not beyond the contrivance of Art, in submersions and Inlays, inverting the extremes of the plant, and fetching the root from the top, and also imitated in handsome columnary work, in the inversion of the extremes; wherein the Capitel, and the Base, hold such near correspondency.

In the motive parts of animals may be discovered mutuall proportions; not only in those of Quadrupeds, but in the thigh-bone, legge, foot-bone, and claws of Birds. The legs of Spiders are made after a sesquitertian proportion, and the long legs of some locusts, double unto some others. But the internodial parts of Vegetables, or spaces between the joints, are contrived with more uncertainty; though the joints themselves in many plants, maintain a regular number.

In vegetable composure, the unition of prominent parts seems most to answer the *Apophyses* or processes of Animall bones, whereof they are the produced parts or prominent explanations. And though in parts of plants which are not ordained for motion, we do not expect correspondent Articulations; yet in the setting on of some flowers, and seeds in their sockets, and the lineal commissure of the pulpe of several seeds, may be observed some shadow of the Harmony; some show of the *Gomphosis* or *mortis*-articulation.

As for the *Diarthrosis* or motive Articulation, there is expected little Analogy, though long-stalked leaves doe move by long lines, and have observable motions, yet are they made by outward impulsion, like the motion of pendulous bodies, while the parts themselves are united by some kind of *symphysis* unto the stock

But standing vegetables, void of motive-Articulations, are not without many motions. For beside the motion of vegetation upward, and of radiation unto all quarters, that of contraction, dilatation, inclination, and contortion, is discoverable in many plants. To omit the rose of Jericho, the ear of Rye, which moves with change of weather, and the Magical spit, made of no rare plants, which windes before the fire, and rosts the bird without turning.

Even Animals near the Classis of plants, seem to have the most restlesse motions. The Summer-worm of Ponds and plashes makes a long waving motion; the hair-worm seldom lies still. He that would behold a very anomalous motion, may observe it in the Tortile and tiring strokes of Gnatworms.[23]

CHAPTER IV

As for the delights, commodities, mysteries, with other concernments of this order, we are unwilling to fly them over, in the short deliveries of Virgil, Varro, or others, and shall therefore enlarge with additional ampliations.

By this position they had a just proportion of Earth, to supply an equality of nourishment. The distance being ordered, thick or thin, according to the magnitude or vigorous attraction of the plant, the goodnesse, leannesse, or propriety of the soyle, and therefore the rule of Solon, concerning the territory of Athens, not extendible unto all; allowing the distance of six foot unto common Trees, and nine for the Figge and Olive.

They had a due diffusion of their roots on both sides, whereby they maintained some proportion to their height, in Trees of large radication. For that they strictly make good their profundeur or depth unto their height, according to common conceit, and that expression of Virgil,[1] though confirmable from the plane Tree in Pliny,[2] and some few examples, is not to be expected from the generation of Trees almost in any kinde, either of side-spreading, or tap-roots: Except we measure them by lateral and opposite diffusions; nor commonly to be found in minor or hearby plants; If we except Sea-holly, Liquorish, Sea-rush, and some others.

They had a commodious radiation in their growth; and a due expansion of their branches, for shadow or delight. For trees thickly planted, do runne up in height and branch with no expansion, shooting unequally or short, and thinne upon the neighbouring side. And therefore Trees are inwardly bare, and spring, and leaf from the outward and Sunny side of their branches.

Whereby they also avoided the peril of συνολεθρισμὸς, or one tree perishing with another, as it happeneth ofttimes from the sick *effluviums* or entanglements of the roots, falling foul with each other. Observable in Elmes set in hedges, where if one dieth the neighbouring Tree prospereth not long after.

In this situation divided into many intervals and open unto six passages, they had the advantage of a fair perflation from windes, brushing and cleansing their surfaces, relaxing and closing their pores unto due perspiration. For that they afford large effluviums perceptible from odours, diffused at great distances, is observable from Onyons out of the earth; which though dry, and kept until the spring, as they shoot forth large and many leaves, do notably abate of their weight. And mint growing in glasses of water, until it arriveth unto the weight of an ounce, in a shady place, will sometimes exhaust a pound of water.

And as they send forth much, so may they receive somewhat in: For beside the common way and road of reception by the root, there may be a refection and imbibition from without; For gentle showrs refresh plants, though they enter not their roots; And the good and bad effluviums of Vegetables, promote or debilitate each other. So *Epithymum* and Dodder, rootlesse and out of the ground, maintain themselves upon Thyme, Savory, and plants, whereon they hang. And Ivy divided from the root, we have observed to live some years, by the cirrous parts commonly conceived but as tenacles and holdfasts unto it. The stalks of mint cropt from the root stripped from the leaves, and set in glasses with the root end upward, & out of the water, we have observed to send forth sprouts and leaves without the aid of roots, and *scordium* to grow in like manner, the leaves set downward in water. To omit severall Sea-plants, which grow on single roots from stones, although in very many there are side-shoots and fibres, beside the fastening root.

By this open position they were fairly exposed unto the rayes of Moon and Sunne, so considerable in the growth of Vegetables. For though Poplars, Willows, and severall Trees be made to grow about the brinks of Acharon, and dark habitations of the dead; Though some plants are content to grow in obscure Wells; wherein also old Elme pumps afford sometimes long bushy sprouts, not observable in any above-ground: And large fields of Vegetables are able to maintain their verdure at the bottome and shady part of the Sea; yet the greatest number are not content without the actual rayes of the Sunne, but bend, incline, and follow them; As large lists of solisequious and Sun-following plants. And some observe the method of its motion in their owne growth and conversion twining towards the West by the South, as Bryony, Hops, Woodbine, and several kindes of Bindeweed, which we shall more admire; when any can tell us, they observe another motion, and Twist by the North at the Antipodes. The same plants rooted against an erect North-wall full of holes, will finde a way through them to look upon the Sunne. And in tender plants from mustard seed, sown in the winter, and in a plot of earth placed inwardly against a South-window, the tender stalks of two leaves arose not erect, but bending towards the window, nor looking much higher then the Meridian Sun. And if the pot were turned they would work themselves into their former declinations, making their conversion by the East. That the Leaves of the Olive and some other Trees solstitially turn, and precisely tell us, when the Sun is entred Cancer, is scarce expectable in any Climate; and Theophrastus warily observes it;[3] Yet somewhat thereof is observable in our own, in the leaves of Willows and Sallows, some weeks after the Solstice. But the great Convolvulus or white-flower'd Bindeweed observes both motions of the Sunne, while the flower twists Æquinoctionally from the left hand to the right, according to the daily revolution; The stalk twineth ecliptically from the right to the left, according to the annual conversion.

Some commend the exposure of these orders unto the Western gales, as the most generative and fructifying breath of heaven. But we applaud the Husbandry of Solomon, whereto agreeth the doctrine of Theophrastus. Arise O North-winde, and blow thou South upon my garden, that the spices thereof may flow out; For the North-winde closing the pores, and shutting up the effluviums, when the South doth after open and relax them; the Aromatical gummes do drop, and sweet odours fly actively from them. And if his garden had the same situation, which mapps, and charts afford it, on the East side of Jerusalem, and having the wall on the West; these were the windes, unto which it was well exposed.

By this way of plantation they encreased the number of their trees, which they lost in *Quaternio's*, and square-orders, which is a commodity insisted on by Varro,[4] and one great intent of nature, in this position of flowers and seeds in the elegant formation of plants, and the former Rules observed in naturall and artificiall Figurations.

Whether in this order and one Tree in some measure breaking the cold, and pinching gusts of windes from the other, trees will not better maintain their inward circles, and either escape or moderate their excentricities, may also be considered. For the circles in Trees are naturally concentricall, parallell unto the bark, and unto each other, till frost and piercing wines contract and close them on the weatherside, the opposite semicircle widely enlarging, and at a comely distance, which hindreth ofttimes the beauty and roundnesse of Trees, and makes the Timber lesse serviceable; whiles the ascending juyce not readily passing, settles in knots and inequalities. And therefore it is no new course of Agriculture, to observe the native position of Trees according to North and South in their transplantations.

The same is also observable underground in the circinations and sphærical rounds of Onyons, wherein the circles of the Orbes are ofttimes larger, and the meridionall lines stand wider upon one side then the other. And where the largenesse will make up the number of planetical Orbes, that of Luna, and the lower planets excede the dimensions of Saturne, and the higher: Whether the like be not verified in the Circles of the large roots of Briony and Mandrakes, or why in the knotts of Deale or Firre the Circles are often eccentricall, although not in a plane, but vertical and right position, deserves a further enquiry.

Whether there be not some irregularity of roundnesse in most plants according to their position? Whether some small compression of pores be not perceptible in parts which stand against the current of waters, as in Reeds, Bullrushes, and other vegetables toward the streaming quarter, may also be observed, and therefore such as are long and weak, are commonly contrived into a roundnesse of figure, whereby the water presseth lesse, and slippeth more smoothly from them, and even in flags of flat-figured leaves, the greater part obvert their sharper sides unto the current in ditches.

But whether plants which float upon the surface of the water, be for the most part of cooling qualities, those which shoot above it of heating vertues, and why? whether Sargasso for many miles floating upon the Western Ocean, or Sea-lettuce, and Phasganium at the bottome of our Seas, make good the like qualities? Why Fenny waters afford the hottest and sweetest plants, as Calamus, Cyperus, and Crowfoot, and mudd cast out of ditches most naturally produceth Arsmart, Why plants so greedy of water so little regard oyl? Why since many seeds contain much oyle within them, they endure it not well without, either in their growth or production? Why since Seeds shoot commonly under ground, and out of the ayre, those which are let fall in shallow glasses, upon the surface of the water, will sooner sprout then those at the bottome? And if the water be covered with oyle, those at the bottome will hardly sprout at all, we have not room to conjecture.

Whether Ivy would not lesse offend the Trees in this clean ordination, and well kept paths, might perhaps deserve the question. But this were a quæry only unto some habitations, and little concerning Cyrus or the Babylonian territory; wherein by no industry Harpalus could make Ivy grow: And Alexander hardly found it about those parts to imitate the pomp of Bacchus.[5] And though in these Northern Regions we are too much acquainted with one Ivy, we know too little of another, whereby we apprehend not the expressions of Antiquity, the Splenetick[6] medicine of Galen, and the Emphasis of the Poet, in the beauty of the white Ivy.[7]

The like concerning the growth of Misseltoe, which dependeth not only of the species, or kinde of Tree, but much also of the Soil. And therefore common in some places, not readily found in others, frequent in France, not so common in Spain, and scarce at all in the Territory of Ferrara: Nor easily to be found where it is most required upon Oaks, lesse on Trees continually verdant. Although in some places the Olive escapeth it not, requiting its detriment, in the delightfull view of its red Berries; as Clusius observed in Spain, and Bellonius about Hierusalem. But this Parasiticall plant suffers nothing to grow upon it, by any way of art; nor could we ever make it grow where nature had not planted it; as we have in vain attempted by inocculation and incision, upon its native or forreign stock. And though there seem nothing improbable in the seed, it hath not succeeded by sation in any manner of ground, wherein we had no reason to despair, since we reade of vegetable horns, and how Rams horns will root about Goa.[8]

But besides these rurall commodities, it cannot be meanly delectable in the variety of Figures, which these orders open, and closed do make. Whilest every inclosure makes a Rhombus, the figures obliquely taken a Rhomboides, the intervals bounded with parallell lines, and each intersection built upon a square, affording two Triangles or Pyramids vertically conjoyned; which in the strict Quincunciall order doe oppositely make acute and blunt Angles.

And though therein we meet not with right angles, yet every Rhombus containing four Angles equall unto two right, it virtually contains two right in every one. Nor is this strange unto such as observe the naturall lines of Trees, and parts disposed in them. For neither in the root doth nature affect this angle, which shooting downward for the stability of the plant, doth best effect the same by Figures of Inclination; Nor in the Branches and stalky leaves, which grow most at acute angles; as declining from their head the root, and diminishing their Angles with their altitude: Verified also in lesser Plants, whereby they better support themselves, and bear not so heavily upon the stalk: So that while near the root they often make an Angle of seventy parts, the sprouts near the top will often come short of thirty. Even in the nerves and master veins of the leaves the acute angle ruleth; the obtuse but seldome found, and in the backward part of the leaf, reflecting and arching about the stalk. But why ofttimes one side of the leaf is unequall unto the other, as in Hazell and Oaks, why on either side the master vein the lesser and derivative channels not directly opposite, nor at equall angles, respectively unto the adverse side, but those of one part do often exceed the other, as the Wallnut and many more deserves another enquiry.

Now if for this order we affect coniferous and tapering Trees, particularly the Cypresse, which grows in a conicall figure; we have found a Tree not only of great Ornament, but in its Essentials of affinity unto this order. A solid Rhombus being made by the conversion of two Equicrurall cones, as Archimedes hath defined. And these were the common Trees about Babylon, and the East, whereof the Ark was made; and Alexander found no Trees so accomodable to build his Navy; And this we rather think to be the Tree mentioned in the Canticles, which stricter Botanology will hardly allow to be Camphire.

And if delight or ornamentall view invite a comely disposure by circular amputations, as is elegantly performed in Hawthorns; then will they answer the figures made by the conversion of a Rhombus, which maketh two concentricall Circles; the greater circumference being made by the lesser angles, the lesser by the greater.

The Cylindrical figure of Trees is virtually contained and latent in this order. A Cylinder or long round being made by the conversion or turning of a Parallelogram, and most handsomely by a long square, which makes an equall, strong and lasting figure in Trees, agreeable unto the body and motive parts of animals, the greatest number of Plants, and almost all roots, though their stalks be angular, and of many corners, which seem not to follow the figure of their Seeds; Since many angular Seeds send forth round stalks, and sphæricall seeds arise from angular spindles, and many rather conform unto their Roots, as the round stalks of bulbous Roots, and in tuberous Roots stemmes of like figure. But why since the largest number of Plants maintain a circular Figure, there are so few with teretous or longround leaves; why coniferous Trees are tenuifolious or narrowleafed, why Plants of few or no joynts have commonly round stalks, why the greatest number of hollow stalks are round stalks; or why in this variety of angular stalks the quadrangular most exceedeth, were too long a speculation; Mean while obvious experience may finde, that in Plants of divided leaves above, nature often beginneth circularly in the two first leaves below, while in the singular plant of Ivy, she exerciseth a contrary Geometry, and beginning with angular leaves below, rounds them in the upper branches.

Nor can the rows in this order want delight, as carrying an aspect answerable unto the *dipteros hypæthros*, or double order of columns open above; the opposite ranks of Trees standing like pillars in the *Cavedia* of the Courts of famous buildings, and the Portico's of the *Templa subdialia* of old; Somewhat imitating the *Peristylia* or Cloyster buildings, and the *Exedræ* of the Ancients, wherein men discoursed, walked and exercised; For that they derived the rule of Columnes from Trees, especially in their proportionall diminutions, is illustrated by Vitruvius from the shaftes of Firre and Pine.[9] And though the inter-arboration do imitate the *Areostylos*, or thin order, not strictly answering the proportion of intercolumniations; yet in many Trees they will not exceed the intermission of the Columnes in the Court of the Tabernacle; which being an hundred cubits long, and made up by twenty pillars, will afford no lesse then intervals of five cubits.

Beside, in this kinde of aspect the sight being not diffused but circumscribed between long parallels and the ἐπισκιασμὸς and adumbration from the branches, it frameth a penthouse over the eye, and maketh a quiet vision: And therefore in diffused and open aspects, men hollow their hand above their eye, and make an artificiall brow, whereby they direct the dispersed rayes of sight, and by this shade preserve a moderate light in the chamber of the eye; keeping the *pupilla* plump and fair, and not contracted or shrunk as in light and vagrant vision.

And therefore providence hath arched and paved the great house of the world, with colours or mediocrity, that is, blew and green, above and below the sight, moderately terminating the *acies* of the eye. For most plants, though green above ground, maintain their Originall white below it, according to the candour of their seminall pulp, and the rudimental leaves do first appear in that colour; observable in Seeds sprouting in water upon their first foliation. Green seeming to be the first supervenient, or above-ground complexion of Vegetables, separable in many upon ligature or inhumation, as Succory, Endive, Artichoaks, and which is also lost upon fading in the Autumn.

And this is also agreeable unto water it self, the alimental vehicle of plants, which first altereth into this colour; And containing many vegetable seminalities, revealeth their Seeds by greennesse; and therefore soonest expected in rain or standing water, not easily found in distilled or water strongly boiled; wherein the

Seeds are extinguished by fire and decoction, and therefore last long and pure without such alteration, affording neither uliginous coats, gnatworms, Acari, hair-worms, like crude and common water; and therefore most fit for wholsome beverage, and with malt makes Ale and Beer without boyling. What large water-drinkers some Plants are, the Canary-Tree and Birches in some Northern Countries, drenching the Fields about them do sufficiently demonstrate. How water it self is able to maintain the growth of Vegetables, and without extinction of their generative or medicall vertues; Beside the experiment of Helmonts tree, we have found in some which have lived six years in glasses. The seeds of Scurvy-grasse growing in waterpots, have been fruitfull in the Land; and Asarum after a years space, and once casting its leaves, hath handsomely performed its vomiting operation.

Nor are only dark and green colors, but shades and shadows contrived through the great Volume of nature, and trees ordained not only to protect and shadow others, but by their shades and shadowing parts, to preserve and cherish themselves. The whole radiation or branchings shadowing the stock and the root, the leaves, the branches and fruit, too much exposed to the windes and scorching Sunne. The calicular leaves inclose the tender flowers, and the flowers themselves lye wrapt about the seeds, in their rudiment and first formations, which being advanced the flowers fall away; and are therefore contrived in variety of figures, best satisfying the intention; Handsomely observable in hooded and gaping flowers, and the Butterfly bloomes of leguminous plants, the lower leaf closely involving the rudimental Cod, and the alary or wingy divisions embracing or hanging over it.

But Seeds themselves do lie in perpetual shades, either under the leaf, or shut up in coverings; And such as lye barest, have their husks, skins, and pulps about them, wherein the nebbe and generative particle lyeth moist and secured from the injury of Ayre and Sunne. Darknesse and light hold interchangeable dominions, and alternately rule the seminall state of things. Light unto Pluto[10] is darknesse unto Jupiter. Legions of seminall Idæa's lye in their second Chaos and Orcus of Hippocrates; till putting on the habits of their forms, they shew themselves upon the stage of the world, and open dominion of Jove. They that held the Stars of heaven were but rayes and flashing glimpses of the Empyreall light, through holes and perforations of the upper heaven, took of the natural shadows of stars, while according to better discovery[11] the poor Inhabitants of the Moone have but a polary life, and must passe half their dayes in the shadow of that Luminary.

Light that makes things seen, makes some things invisible, were it not for darknesse and the shadow of the earth, the noblest part of the Creation had remained unseen, and the Stars in heaven as invisible as on the fourth day, when they were created above the Horizon, with the Sun, or there was not an eye to behold them. The greatest mystery of Religion is expressed by adumbration, and in the noblest part of Jewish Types, we finde the Cherubims shadowing the Mercy-seat:[12] Life it self is but the shadow of death, and souls departed but the shadows of the living: All things fall under this name. The Sunne it self is but the dark *simulachrum*, and light but the shadow of God.

Lastly, It is no wonder that this Quincunciall order was first and still affected as gratefull unto the Eye: For all things are seen Quincuncially; For at the eye the Pyramidal rayes from the object, receive a decussation, and so strike a second base upon the Retina or hinder coat, the proper organ of Vision; wherein the pictures from objects are represented, answerable to the paper, or wall in the dark chamber; after the decussation of the rayes at the hole of the hornycoat, and their refraction upon the Christalline humour, answering the *foramen* of the window, and the convex or burning-glasses, which refract the rayes that enter it. And if ancient Anatomy would hold, a like disposure there was of the optick or visual nerves in the brain, wherein Antiquity conceived a concurrence by decussation. And this not only observable in the laws of direct Vision, but in some part also verified in the reflected rayes of sight. For making the angle of incidence equal to that of reflexion, the visuall raye returneth Quincuncially, and after the form of a V, and the line of reflexion being continued unto the place of vision, there ariseth a semi-decussation, which makes the object seen in a perpendicular unto it self, and as farre below the reflectent, as it is from it above; observable in the Sun and Moon beheld in water.

And this is also the law of reflexion in moved bodies and sounds, which though not made by decussation, observe the rule of equality between incidence and reflexion; whereby whispering places are framed by Ellipticall arches laid side-wise; where the voice being delivered at the focus of one extremity, observing an equality unto the angle of incidence, it will reflect unto the focus of the other end, and so escape the ears of the standers in the middle.

A like rule is observed in the reflection of the vocall and sonorous line in Ecchoes, which cannot therefore be heard in all stations. But happening in woody plantations, by waters, and able to return some words; if reacht by a pleasant and well-dividing voice, there may be heard the softest notes in nature.

And this not only verified in the way of sence, but in animall and intellectuall receptions. Things entring upon the intellect by a Pyramid from without, and thence into the memory by another from within, the common decussation being in the understanding as is delivered by Bovillus.[13] Whether the intellectual and phantastical lines be not thus rightly disposed, but magnified diminished, distorted, and ill placed in the Mathematicks of some brains, whereby they have irregular apprehensions of things, perverted motions, conceptions, incurable hallucinations, were no unpleasant speculation.

And if Ægyptian Philosophy may obtain, the scale of influences was thus disposed, and the geniall spirits of both worlds, do trace their way in ascending and descending Pyramids, mystically apprehended in the Letter X, and the open Bill and stradling Legges of a Stork, which was imitated by that Character.

Of this Figure Plato[14] made choice to illustrate the motion of the soul, both of the world and man; while he delivereth that God divided the whole conjunction length-wise, according to the figure of a Greek X, and then turning it about reflected it into a circle; By the circle implying the uniform motion of the first Orb, and by the right lines, the planetical and various motions within it. And this also with application unto the soul of man, which hath a double aspect, one right, whereby it beholdeth the body, and objects without; another circular and reciprocal, whereby it beholdeth it self. The circle declaring the motion of the indivisible soul, simple, according to the divinity of its nature, and returning into it self; the right lines respecting the motion pertaining unto sense, and vegetation, and the central decussation, the wondrous connexion of the severall faculties conjointly in one substance. And so conjoyned the unity and duality of the soul, and made out the three substances so much considered by him; That is, the indivisible or divine, the divisible or corporeal, and that third, which was the *Systasis* or harmony of those two, in the mystical decussation.

And if that were clearly made out which Justin Martyr took for granted, this figure hath had the honour to characterize and notifie our blessed Saviour, as he delivereth in that borrowed expression from Plato; *Decussavit eum in universo*, the hint whereof he would have Plato derive from the figure of the brazen Serpent, and to have mistaken the Letter X for T, whereas it is not improbable, he learned these and other mystical expressions in his Learned Observations of Ægypt, where he might obviously behold the Mercurial characters, the handed crosses, and other mysteries not throughly understood in the sacred Letter X, which being derivative from the Stork, one of the ten sacred animals, might be originally Ægyptian, and brought into Greece by Cadmus of that Countrey.

CHAPTER V

The Quincunx Mystically Considered

To enlarge this contemplation unto all the mysteries and secrets, accomodable unto this number, were inexcusable Pythagorisme, yet cannot omit the ancient conceit of five surnamed the number of justice;[1] as justly dividing between the digits, and hanging in the centre of Nine, described by square numeration, which angularly divided will make the decussated number; and so agreeable unto the Quincunciall Ordination, and rowes divided by Equality, and just decorum, in the whole complantation; And might be the Originall of that common game among us, wherein the fifth place is Soveraigne, and carrieth the chief intention. The Ancients wisely instructing youth, even in their recreations unto virtue, that is, early to drive at the middle point and Central Seat of justice.

Nor can we omit how agreeable unto this number an handsome division is made in Trees and Plants, since Plutarch, and the Ancients have named it the Divisive Number, justly dividing the Entities of the world, many remarkable things in it, and also comprehending the general division of Vegetables.[2] And he that considers how most blossomes of Trees, and greatest number of Flowers, consist of five leaves; and therein doth rest the setled rule of nature; So that in those which exceed there is often found, or easily made a variety; may readily discover how nature rests in this number, which is indeed the first rest and pause of numeration in the fingers, the naturall Organs thereof. Nor in the division of the feet of perfect animals doth nature exceed this account. And even in the joints of feet, which in birds are most multiplied, surpasseth not this number; So progressionally making them out in many, that from five in the fore-claw she descendeth unto two in the hindemost; And so in fower feet makes up the number of joynts, in the five fingers or toes of man.

Not to omit the Quintuple Section of a Cone,[3] of handsome practice in Ornamentall Garden-plots, and in some way discoverable in so many works of Nature; In the leaves, fruits, and seeds of Vegetables, and scales of some Fishes, so much considerable in glasses, and the optick doctrine; wherein the learned may consider the Crystalline humour of the eye in the cuttle fish and *Loligo*.

He that forgets not how Antiquity named this the Conjugall or Wedding number, made it the Embleme of the most remarkable conjunction, will conceive it duely appliable unto this handsome Oeconomy, and vegetable combination; May hence apprehend the allegorical sence of that obscure expression of Hesiod,[4] and afford no improbable reason why Plato admitted his Nuptiall guests by fives, in the kindred of the married couple.[5]

And though a sharper mystery might be implied in the Number of the five wise and foolish Virgins, which were to meet the Bridegroom, yet was the same agreeable unto the Conjugall Number, which ancient Numerists made out by two and three, the first parity and imparity, the active and passive digits, the materiall and formall principles in generative Societies. And not discordant even from the customes of the Romans, who admitted but five[6] torches in their Nuptiall solemnities. Whether there were any mystery or not implied, the most generative animals were created on this day, and had accordingly the largest benediction: And under a Quintuple consideration, wanton Antiquity considered the Circumstances of generation, while by this number of five they naturally divided the Nectar of the fifth Planet.

The same number in the Hebrew mysteries and Cabalistical accounts was the character[7] of Generation; declared by the letter He, the fifth in their Alphabet; According to that Cabalisticall Dogma: If Abram had not had this Letter added unto his Name he had remained fruitlesse, and without the power of generation: Not onely because hereby the number of his Name attained two hundred fourty eight, the number of the affirmative precepts, but because as in created natures there is a male and female, so in divine and intelligent productions, the mother of Life and Fountain of souls in Cabalisticall Technology is called *Binah*; whose Seal and Character was *He*. So that being sterill before, he received the power of generation from that measure and mansion in the Archetype; and was made conformable unto Binah. And upon such involved considerations, the ten[8] of Sarai was exchanged into five, If any shall look upon this as a stable number, and fitly appropriable unto Trees, as Bodies of Rest and Station, he hath herein a great Foundation in nature, who observing much variety in legges and motive Organs of Animals, as two, four, six, eight, twelve, fourteen, and more, hath passed over five and ten, and assigned them unto none.[9] And for the stability of this Number, he shall not want the sphericity of its nature, which multiplied in it self, will return into its own denomination, and bring up the reare of the account. Which is also one of the Numbers that makes up the mysticall Name of God, which consisting of Letters denoting all the sphæricall Numbers, ten, five, and six; Emphatically sets forth the Notion of Trismegistus, and that intelligible Sphere, which is the Nature of God.

Many Expressions by this Number occurre in Holy Scripture, perhaps unjustly laden with mysticall Expositions, and little concerning our order. That the Israelites were forbidden to eat the fruit of their newly planted Trees, before the fifth yeare, was very agreeable unto the naturall Rules of Husbandry: Fruits being unwholsome and lash before the fourth, or fifth Yeare. In the second day or Feminine or very few, as the Phalangium monstrosum Brasilianum, Clusii & Jac. De Laet. Cur. poster. Americæ Descript.If perfectly described. part of five, there was added no approbation. For in the third or masculine day, the same is twice repeated; and a double benediction inclosed both Creations, whereof the one, in some part was but an accomplishment of the other. That the Trespasser[10] was to pay a fifth part above the head or principall, makes no secret in this Number, and implied no more then one part above the principall; which being considered in four parts, the additionall forfeit must bear the Name of a fift. The five golden mice had plainly their determination from the number of the Princes; That five should put to flight an hundred might have nothing mystically implyed; considering a rank of Souldiers could scarce consist of a lesser number. Saint Paul had rather speak five words in a known then ten thousand in an unknowne tongue: That is as little as could well be spoken. A simple proposition consisting of three words and a complexed one not ordinarily short of five.

More considerable there are in this mysticall account, which we must not insist on. And therefore why the radicall Letters in the Pentateuch, should equall the number of the Souldiery of the Tribes; Why our Saviour in the Wildernesse fed five thousand persons with five Barley Loaves, and again, but four thousand with no lesse then seven of Wheat? Why Joseph designed five changes of Rayment unto Benjamin? and David took just five pibbles out of the Brook against the Pagan Champion? We leave it unto Arithmeticall Divinity, and Theologicall explanation.

Yet if any delight in new Problemes, or think it worth the enquiry, whether the Criticall Physician hath rightly hit the nominall notation of Quinque;[11] Why the Ancients mixed five or three but not four parts of water into their Wine: And Hippocrates observed a fifth proportion in the mixture of water with milk, as in Dysenteries and bloudy fluxes. Under what abstruse foundation Astrologers do Figure the good or bad Fate from our Children, in a good Fortune,[12] or the fifth house of their Celestiall Schemes. Whether the Ægyptians described a Starre by a Figure of five points, with reference unto the five Capitall aspects,[13]whereby they transmit their Influences, or abstruser Considerations? Why the Cabalisticall Doctors, who conceive the whole *Sephiroth*, or divine emanations to have guided the ten-stringed Harp of David, whereby he pacified the evil spirit of Saul, in strict numeration doe begin with the Perihypate Meson, or ff fa ut, and so place the Tiphereth answering C sol fa ut, upon the fifth string: Or whether this number be oftner applied unto bad things and ends, then good in holy Scripture, and why? He may meet with abstrusities of no ready resolution.

If any shall question the rationality of that Magick, in the cure of the blind man by Serapis, commanded to place five fingers on his Altar, and then his hand on his Eyes? Why since the whole Comoedy is primarily and naturally comprised in four[14] parts, and Antiquity permitted not so many persons to speak in one Scene, yet would not comprehend the same in more or lesse then five acts? Why amongst Sea-starres nature chiefly delighteth in five points? And since there are found some of no fewer then twelve, and some of seven, and nine, there are few or none discovered of six or eight? If any shall enquire why the Flowers of Rue properly consist of four Leaves, the first and third have five? Why since many Flowers have one leaf or none,[15] as Scaliger will have it, diverse three, and the greatest number consist of five divided from their bottomes; there are yet so few of two: or why nature generally beginning or setting out with two opposite leaves at the Root, doth so seldome conclude with that order and number at the Flower? he shall not passe his hours in vulgar speculation.

If any shall further quæry why magneticall Philosophy excludeth decussations, and needles transversly placed do naturally distract their verticities? Why Geomancers do imitate the Quintuple Figure, in their Mother Characters of Acquisition and Amission, &c somewhat answering the Figures in the Lady or speckled Beetle? With what Equity, Chiromantical conjecturers decry these decussations in the Lines and Mounts of the hand? What that decussated Figure intendeth in the medall of Alexander the Great? Why the Goddesses sit commonly crosse-legged in ancient draughts, Since Juno is described in the same as a veneficial posture to hinder the birth of Hercules? If any shall doubt why at the Amphidromicall Feasts, on the fifth day after the Childe was born, presents were sent from friends, of *Polipusses*, and Cuttle-fishes? Why five must be only left in that Symbolicall mutiny among the men of Cadmus? Why Proteus in Homer the Symbole of the first matter, before he setled himself in the midst of his Sea-monsters, doth place them out by fives? Why the fifth years Oxe was acceptable Sacrifice unto Jupiter? Or why the Noble Antoninus in some sence doth call the soul it self a Rhombus? He shall not fall on trite or triviall disquisitions. And these we invent and propose unto acuter enquirers, nauseating crambe verities and questions over-queried. Flat and flexible truths are beat out by every hammer; But Vulcan and his whole forge sweat to work out Achilles his armour. A large field is yet left unto sharper discerners to enlarge upon this order, to search out the quaternio's and figured draughts of this nature, and moderating the study of names, and meer nomenclature of plants, to erect generalities, disclose unobserved proprieties, not only in the vegetable shop, but the whole volume of nature; affording delightful Truths, confirmable by sense and ocular Observation, which seems to me the surest path, to trace the Labyrinth of Truth. For though discursive enquiry and rationall conjecture, may leave handsome gashes and flesh-wounds; yet without conjunction of this expect no mortal or dispatching blows unto errour.

But the Quincunx[16] of Heaven runs low, and 'tis time to close the five ports of knowledge; We are unwilling to spin out our awaking thoughts into the phantasmes of sleep, which often continueth præcogitations; making Cables of Cobwebbes and Wildernesses of handsome Groves. Beside Hippocrates[17] hath spoke so little and the Oneirocriticall [18] Masters, have left such frigid Interpretations from plants, that there is little encouragement to dream of Paradise it self. Nor will the sweetest delight of Gardens afford much comfort in sleep; wherein the dulnesse of that sense shakes hands with delectable odours; and though in the Bed[19] of Cleopatra, can hardly with any delight raise up the ghost of a Rose.

Night which Pagan Theology could make the daughter of Chaos, affords no advantage to the description of order: Although no lower then that Masse can we derive its Genealogy. All things began in order, so shall they end, and so shall they begin again; according to the ordainer of order and mystical Mathematicks of the City of Heaven.

Though *Somnus* in Homer be sent to rowse up Agamemnon, I finde no such effects in these drowsy approaches of sleep. To keep our eyes open longer were but to act our Antipodes. The Huntsmen are up in America, and they are already past their first sleep in Persia. But who can be drowsie at that howr which freed us from everlasting sleep? or have slumbring thoughts at that time, when sleep it self must end, as some conjecture all shall awake again?

NOTES

Dedicatory

1. *Plempius, Cabeus*, &c.
2. Dr. Harvey.
3. Besleri *Hortus Eystensis*.
4. Bauhini *Theatrum Botanicum*, &c.
5. My worthy friend M. *Godier*, an ancient and learned Botanist.
6. As in *London* and divers parts, whereof we mention none, lest we seem to omit any.
7. *Hippocrates de superfoetatione, de dentitione.*
8. Rules without exceptions. Alludes to "Postremo, U finita producuntur omnia", 'all final u's are long'.
9. Tulipomania, Narrencruiid, Lauremberg, Pet. Hondius in lib. Belg.
10. Alluding to his joining this *tract* to his *Hydriotaphia*.
11. 'No word without consent of approval'(Seneca, Moral Letters, cxiv, 12.)
12. Of the most worthy Sr Edmund Bacon, prime Baronet, my true and noble Friend.

Chapter I

1. Plato in Timæo.
2.. fronde tegi silvas. [Ovid. Metmorph. I, 44.]
3.. διάρεσις, in opening the flesh, ἐξαίρεσις, in taking out the rib. σὺνϑεσις in closing up the part again.
4.. For some there is from the ambiguity of the word Mikedem, whether ab oriente or a principio. [Genesis 8.2]
5. {Wilkin notes the following passage from the Browne MS. Sloan 1847, "evidently intended for this work": "We are unwilling to diminish or loose the credit of Paradise, or only pass it over with Eden, though the Greek be of a later name. In this excepted, we know not whether the ancient gardens do equal those of late times, or those at present in Europe. Of the gardens of Herperies, we know nothing singular, but some golden apples. Of Alcinous his garden, we read nothing beyond figgs, apples, and olives; if we allow it to be any more than a fiction of Homer, unhappily placed in Corfu, where the sterility of the soil makes men believe there was no such thing at all. The gardens of Adonis were so empty that they afforded proverbial expression, and the principal part thereof was empty spaces, with herbs and flowers in pots. I think we little understand the pensile gardens of Semiramis, which made one of the wonders of it, wherein probably the structure exceeded the plants contained in them. The excellency thereof was probably in the trees, and if the descension of the roots be equal to the height of trees, it was not [absurd] of Strebæus to think the pillars were hollow that the roots might shoot into them."}
6. Josephus. [Ant. Jud. X.11.1, quoting Berosus.]
7. Shushan in Susiana [or Susa; Esther 1.5].
8. Plutarch in the life of Artaxerxes. [Chapter 1]
9.. Xenophon in Oeconomico [IV, 21: see next note].
10. Καλὰ μὲν τά δένδρα, δί ἰσου δε τὰ πεφυτευμένας ὀρθοι δε ὁι στίχοι τῶν δένδρων, ἐυδιώνια δε πάντα καλῶς.

11. Cicero in Cat. Major. [That is, "quincunx"; de Senuctete, XVII.59.]

12.. Benedict Curtius de Hortis. Bapt. porta in villa.

13.. Of Marius, Alexander, Roma Sotteranea.

14. Wherein the lower part is somewhat longer, as defined by Upton de studio militari, and Johannes de Bado Aureo, cum comment. clariss. & doctiss. Bissæi.

15. Casal. de Ritibus. Bosio nella Trionfante croce.

16. Decussatio ipsa jucundum ac peramænum conspectum præbuit. Cart. Hortar. l.6. [Sic, for Curt. Hortor.

17. ὄρχοι, στίχοι ἀμπέων, φυτῶν στίχος, ἡ χατὰ τάξιν φθτεία. Phavorinus Philoxenus

18. ουστάδας ἀμπέλων. Polit. 7

19. Vet. Testamenti Pharus.

20.. Which King Numa set up with his fingers so disposed that they numerically denoted 365. Pliny

Chapter II

1. Of a structure five parts, Fundamentum, parietes, Aperturæ, Compartitio, tectum, Leo. Alberti. Five Columes, Tuscan, Dorick, Ionick, Corinthian, Compound. Five different intercolumniations, Pycnostylos, dystylos, Systylos, Areostylos, Eustylos. Vitru. [Vitruvius III.3]

2. Uti constat ex pergamena apud Chifflet; in in [sic] B. R. Bruxelli, & Icon. f. Stradæ.

3. Macc. 1.11.[13. "Then Ptolemee entered into Antioch, where he set two crowns upon his head, the crown of Asia, and of Egypt."]

4. Arist. Mechan. Quæst.

5. δικτυωταί.

6. In Leviticus

7. Ἄσβεστος δ᾽αρ ἐνῶρτο γέλως. Hom. in Eust. Comm. From *Iliad,* I.599.

8. De armis Scaccatis, masculatis, invectis suselatis vide Spelm. Aspilog. & Upton, cum erudid.

9. As in the contention between Minerva and Arachne. [Ovid. Metamorph. VI]

10. In Eustachius [Sc. Eustathius; see also Chapter I. Eustachius is a different person. On pentalithismus, see Smith's Dictionary s.v. Talus.]

11. Plato. Phaedrus (274)

12. In the disposure of the Legions in the Wars of the Republike, before the division of the Legion into ten Cohorts by the Emperours. Salmas. in his Epistle a Mounsieur de Peyresc. & de Re militari Romanorum.

13. Polybius Appianus.

14. Agathius Ammianus [Naßes: sc. Narses. See Encyclopædia Britannica, s.v. Narses.]

15. Aelian. Tact.

16. ἐν πλαισίῳ. (Thucydides, VI, lxvii, 1 and VII, lxxviii, 2)

17. Diod. Sic. [II.3.2-4]

18. *Antonio Agostino delle medaglie.* The Agostino Medallion

19. Aristot. Mechan.

20. Plut. in vit. Thes. (XXVII.6).

Chapter III

1. Capitula squamata quercuum, Bauhini, whereof though he saith perraro reperiuntur bis tantum invenimus, yet we find them commonly with us and in great numbers.

2. ἔνδον ἐμῶν λαγόνων, μητρὸς ἔχω

3. Antho. Græc. inter Epigrammata γριφῶδη ἐνδὸν ἐμῶν μετρὸς λαγώναν ἔχω πατέρα.

4. Especially the porus cervinus Imperari, Sporosa, or Alga πλατύκερως. Bauhini.

5. There being a single Maggot found almost in every head.

6. Stratiotes [aloides; Greek "stratos", an army, "strategos", a general ("a militarie name from Greece"). The fruits (and the flowers) are hexagonous. The marginal note in 165 is numbered "e" and reads "Strutiotes".]

7. From the Latin *Favus*, a honeycomb.

8. In met. cum Cabeo. [Meteorologica, IV, 3, with Cabeus's commentary.]

9. These and more to be found upon our Oaks.

10. Schoneveldus de Pisc.

11. Doctissim. Laurenburg hort.

12. The long and tender Capricornus rarely found, we could never meet with but two.

13. Which exceedeth not five.

14. Elem. li. 4.

15. Gom. de Sale.

16. Elegantly conspicuous on the inside of the stripped skins of Dive-Fowl, of the Cormorant, Goshonder, Weasell, Loon, &c.

17. Cruces ansatæ, being held by a finger in the circle.

18. Magnus venter, reticulum, omasus, abomasus. – Aristot.

19. 1652. Pseudo. Epidem. Edit. 3 [Book III, Chapter XXVI.]

20. Orchis Anthropophora, Fabii Columne.

21. Socketed, as teeth in the jaw; as opposed to diarthrosis later in the text, connected by joints.

22. Suet. in vit. Aug.

23. Found often in some form of redmaggot in the standing waters of Cisterns in the Summer.

Chapter IV

1. Quantum vertice ad auras Æthereas, tantum radice ad tartara tendit. (Vergil Æneid 445-46).

2. Pliny Historia Naturalis XII.v.9.

3. Theophrastus, Enquiry into Plants, I.X.

4. Varro de Re Rustica I.7.

5. Plutarch, Alexander 5.35.15.

6. Galen de med. secundum loc.

7. Hedera formosior alba. Virgil, Eclogues VII, 38.

8. Linschoten.

9. Vitruvius, V.1.3.

10. Lux orco, tenebræ Jovi, tenebra orco, lux Jovi. Hippocr. de diæta.

11. S. Hevelii Selenographia.

12. On the Ark of the Covenant (Hebrews 9:5).
13. Car. Bovillus de intellectu.
14. In *Timaeus*.

Chapter V

1. δίκη.s
2. Δένδρον, Θάμνος, Φρύγανον, Πόα, Arbor, frutex, suffrutex, herba, and that fifth which comprehendeth the fungi and tubera, whether to be named Ἄσχιον or γύμνον, comprehending also the conferva marina salsa, and Sea-cords, of so many yards length.
3. Elleipsis, parabola, Hyperbole, Circulus, Triangulum.
4. πέμπτας id est nuptias multas Rhodig. [Hesiod WD 802]
5. Plato de leg. 6.
6. Plutarch problem. Rom. [Qu. Rom. 2]
7. Archang. Dog. Cabal. (Archangelus Burgonovus)
8. *Yod* into *He*. [Sara(i) to Sara(h); *yod* is the tenth letter of the Hebrew alphabet, *he* the fifth.(Genesis 17:15).
9. or very few, as the *Phalangium monstrosum Brasilianum, Clusii & Jac. De Laet. Cur. poster. Americæ Descript*. If perfectly described.
10. Lev. 6 :5.
11.τέσσερα ἔνχε four and one, or five, Scalig.
12. Ἀγαθὴ τυχὴ or bona fortuna the name of the fifth house.
13. Conjunct, opposite, sextile, trigonal (trine), tetragonal (square).
14. Πρότασις, ἐπίτασις, κατάστασις, καταστροφή.
15. Unifolium, nullifolium.
16. Hyades near the Horizon about midnight, at that time.
17. De Insomniis.
18. Artemodorus & Apomazar (both wrote treatises on interpreting dreams)
19. Strewed with roses.

THE STATIONER TO THE READER
1658

I cannot omit to advertise, that a Book was published not long since, Entituled, *Natures Cabinet Unlockt*, bearing the Name of this Authour: If any man have been benefited thereby, this Authour is not so ambitious as to challenge the honour thereof, as having no hand in that Work. To distinguish of true and spurious Peeces was the Originall Criticisme, and some were so handsomely counterfeited, that the Entitled Authours needed not to disclaime them. But since it is so, that either he must write himself, or Others will write for him, I know no better Prevention then to act his own part with lesse intermission of his Pen.

AZILOTH ▌▐ BOOKS

Aziloth Books publishes a wide range of titles ranging from hard-to-find esoteric books - *Parchment Books* - to classic works on fiction, politics and philosophy - *Cathedral Classics*. Our newest venture is *Aziloth Books Children's Classics*, with vibrant new covers and illustrations to complement some of the world's very best children's tales. All our imprints are offered to the reader at a competitive price and through as many mediums and outlets as possible.

 We are committed to excellent book production and strive, whenever possible, to add value to our titles with original images, maps and author introductions. With the premium on space in most modern dwellings, we also endeavour - within the limits of good book design - to make our products as slender as possible, allowing more books to be fitted into a given bookshelf area.

We are a small, approachable company and would love to hear any of your comments and suggestions on our plans, products, or indeed on absolutely anything.

Aziloth Books, Rimey Law, Rookhope, Co. Durham, DL13 2BL, England.
t: 01388-517600 e: info@azilothbooks.com w: www.azilothbooks.com

PARCHMENT BOOKS enshrines the concept of the oneness of all true religious traditions - that "the light shines from many different lanterns". Our list below offers titles from both eastern and western spiritual traditions, including Christian, Judaic, Islamic, Daoist, Hindu and Buddhist mystical texts, as well as books on alchemy, hermeticism, paganism, etc..

By bringing together such spiritual texts, we hope to make esoteric and occult knowledge more readily available to those ready to receive it. We do not publish grimoires or titles pertaining to the left hand path. Titles include:

The Prophet	Khalil Gibran
The Madman: His Parables & Poems	Khalil Gibran
Abandonment to Divine Providence	Jean-Pierre de Caussade
Corpus Hermeticum	G. R. S. Mead (trans.)
The Holy Rule of St Benedict	St. Benedict of Nursia
The Confession of St Patrick	St. Patrick
The Outline of Sanity	G. K. Chesterton
An Outline of Occult Science	Rudolf Steiner
The Dialogue Of St Catherine Of Siena	St. Catherine of Siena
Esoteric Christianity; Thought-Forms*	Annie Besant
The Teachings of Zoroaster	Shapurji A. Kapadia
The Spiritual Exercises of St. Ignatius	St. Ignatius of Loyola
Daemonologie	King James of England
A Dweller on Two Planets	Phylos the Thibetan
Bushido*	Nitobe Inazo
The Interior Castle	St. Teresa of Avila
Songs of Innocence & Experience*	William Blake
The Secret of the Rosary	St. Louis Marie de Montfort
From Ritual to Romance	Jessie L. Weston
The God of the Witches	Margaret Murray
Kundalini – an occult experience	George S. Arundale
The Kingdom of God is Within You	Leo Tolstoy
The Trial and Death of Socrates	Plato
A Textbook of Theosophy	Charles W. Leadbetter
Chuang Tzu: Daoist Teachings	Chuang Tzu
Practical Mysticism	Evelyn Underhill
Tao Te Ching (Lao Tzu's 'Book of the Way')	Tzu, Lao
The Most Holy Trinosophia	Le Comte de St.-Germain
Tertium Organum	P. D. Ouspensky
Totem and Taboo	Sigmund Freud
The Kebra Negast	E. A. Wallis Budge
Esoteric Buddhism	Alfred Percy Sinnett
Demian: the story of a youth	Hermann Hesse

* with colour illustrations

Obtainable at all good online and local bookstores.
View Aziloth Books' full list at: www.azilothbooks.com

CATHEDRAL CLASSICS hosts an array of classic literature, from erudite ancient tomes to avant-garde, twentieth-century masterpieces, all of which deserve a place in your home.　All the world's great novelists are here, Jane Austen, Dickens, Conrad, Arthur Machen and Henry James, brushing shoulders with such disparate luminaries as Sun Tzu, Marcus Aurelius, Kipling, Friedrich Nietzsche, Machiavelli, and Omar Khayam.　A small selection is detailed below:

Frankenstein	Mary Shelley
Herland; With Her in Ourland	Charlotte Perkins Gilman
The Time Machine; The Invisible Man	H. G. Wells
Three Men in a Boat	Jerome K Jerome
The Rubaiyat of Omar Khayyam	Omar Khayyam
A Study in Scarlet	Arthur Conan Doyle
The Sign of the Four	Arthur Conan Doyle
The Picture of Dorian Gray	Oscar Wilde
Flatland	Edwin A. Abbott
The Coming Race	Bulwer Lytton
The Adventures of Sherlock Holmes	Arthur Conan Doyle
The Great God Pan	Arthur Machen
Beyond Good and Evil	Friedrich Nietzsche
England, My England	D. H. Lawrence
The Castle of Otranto	Horace Walpole
Self-Reliance, & Other Essays (series1&2)	Ralph W. Emmerson
The Art of War	Sun Tzu
A Shepherd's Life	W. H. Hudson
The Double	Fyodor Dostoyevsky
To the Lighthouse; Mrs Dalloway	Virginia Woolf
The Sorrows of Young Werther	Johann W. Goethe
Leaves of Grass - 1855 edition	Walt Whitman
Analects	Confucius
Beowulf	Anonymous
Plain Tales From The Hills	Rudyard Kipling
The Subjection of Women	John Stuart Mill
The Rights of Man	Thomas Paine
Progress and Poverty	Henry George
Captain Blood	Rafael Sabatini
Captains Courageous	Rudyard Kipling
The Meditations of Marcus Aurelius	Marcus Aurelius
The Social Contract	Jean Jacques Rousseau
War is a Racket	Smedley D. Butler
The Dead	James Joyce
The Old Wives' Tale	Arnold Bennett
Letters Concerning the English Nation	Voltaire

Obtainable at all good online and local bookstores.
View Aziloth Books' full list at: www.azilothbooks.com

Aziloth Books is passionate about bringing the very best in children's classics fiction to the next generation of book-lovers. We believe in the transforming power of children's books to encourage a life-long love of reading, and publish only the best authors and illustrators. With its original design and outstanding quality, our highly successful list has something to suit every age and interest. Titles include:

The Railway Children	Edith Nesbit
Anne of Green Gables	Lucy Maud Montgomery
What Katy Did	Susan Coolidge
Puck of Pook's Hill	Rudyard Kipling
The Jungle Books	Rudyard Kipling
Just So Stories	Rudyard Kipling
Alice Through the Looking Glass	Charles Dodgson
*Alice's Adventures in Wonderland**	Charles Dodgson
Black Beauty	Anna Sewell
The War of the Worlds	H. G Wells
The Time Machine	H. G .Wells
The Sleeper Awakes	H. G. Wells
The Invisible Man	H. G. Wells
The Lost World	Sir Arthur Conan Doyle
*Gulliver's Travels**	Jonathan Swift
Catriona (David Balfour)	Robert Louis Stevenson
The Water Babies	Charles Kingsley
The First Men in the Moon	Jules Verne
The Secret Garden	Frances Hodgson Burnett
A Little Princess	Frances Hodgson Burnett
*Peter Pan**	J. M. Barrie
*The Song of Hiawatha**	Henry W. Longfellow
Tales from Shakespeare	Charles and Mary Lamb
The Wonderful Wizard of Oz	L. Frank Baum

*with colour illustrations

Obtainable at all good online and local bookstores.
View Aziloth Books' full list at: www.azilothbooks.com

www.ingramcontent.com/pod-product-compliance
Lightning Source LLC
Chambersburg PA
CBHW071617040426
42452CB00009B/1371